AF572651

Outrace the Dawn

Francis S. Hewitt

Outrace The Dawn

Collected Poems
1925 – 1989

The Belvedere Press
Arlington

Published by The Belvedere Press, 4908 Washington Boulevard,
Arlington, Virginia 22205

Library of Congress Cataloging-in-Publication Data

Hewitt, Francis S., 1909 – 1990.
Outrace the dawn : collected poems, 1925 – 1989 / by
Francis S. Hewitt. — 1st ed.
p. cm.
ISBN 0-911057-03-X
I. Title.
PS3558.E827A17 1994 93-35946
811'.54 — dc20 CIP

Printed in the United States of America

FOR MARY,
WHO HAS MADE POETRY
OUT OF LIVING

Contents

FROM 1930 TO 1933

FROM 1941 TO 1954

FROM 1960 TO 1968

FROM 1980 TO 1989

PREFACE

Francis Hewitt's poetry grew out of his experiences and observations. At twenty, as he spent carefree days with friends at New Jersey's shore, he also meticulously recorded in a notebook the spoken phrases, humorous experiences, names of movies and songs he wanted to remember—and why.

The "Memory Lane" series shows the writer as a young man, tuning his eye and ear, honing his skills of observations and note-taking. A lifetime of writing followed.

The volume's title, OUTRACE THE DAWN, appears in *Testament to Marilyn,* written to his infant daughter during World War II army service.

Poems are arranged for the most part in chronological order by decades. Often the author had recorded the month, day, and year of the work. In some instances where a poem lacked a date, family members have been able to place it within a time frame.

His vocabulary was vast. Knowing that he could summon just the right word for its meaning or rhythm, he felt assured enough to play with words. His spelling, punctuation, and indentation have been retained.

As a boy he had heard stories of his grandfather, a seaman, and of his uncle, a lighthouse keeper. In his poetic memory bank, he stored his own sights, smells, and sounds of the shore. The sea became the subject for some of his major poems—*Five Mile Beach* and *The Wreck of the Nancy Lee.* Sea-inspired imagery appears in countless others.

The Author's Notes about his poems give the reader insight into his creative process. One poem's evolution stretched over years; another poem seemed to write itself quickly.

While a loving husband, father and grandfather, a Rutgers teacher and a Senate Appropriations Committee director, a neighbor and a friend, Francis Hewitt was always a writer.

Celebrating his memory at the 1990 memorial service, Dr. Michael Rivkin, a family friend, said: "His memory is a cloak made of the softest, richest wool which when wrapped about, warms against winter's wind on a gray December day, reminding us of Spring's warm sunlight which lies ahead."

Francis S. Hewitt: the poet, the man.

—The Editor

The Hereford Inlet Lighthouse in historic Cape May County, New Jersey, was established in 1874. Located on Five Mile Beach in North Wildwood, this picturesque Victorian structure inspired the author's poem *"Five Mile Beach."*

Captain Freeling H. Hewitt, the author's uncle, was lighthouse keeper from 1878 until 1918. Edwin Hewitt, now Keeper of the Light, is the author's cousin.

Hereford Inlet Lighthouse is listed in the National Registry of Historic Places.

OUTRACE THE DAWN

From 1925 to 1929

Our Gang

As the years go rolling by
And our chums drift far apart,
Each of us will heave a sigh
For that gang, deep in our heart.

Remember how we all came
Down to Skinner's after school
And played Stop, that good old game,
A'fighting over every rule?

How we had such nifty fun
In Marbles where we staged bull-fights?
Ready always in flight to run
As soon as one a copper sights?

Vacation days were spent by all
Playing tennis at the courts;
Watching, while we lobbed the ball,
Above for falling booze by quarts!

Harry, Joe, Kid, and France
George, Al, Chink, and Charlie,
Each remembered when by chance
Some face renews our memory.

May 1925

Green Years: Vignettes of Childhood

I

Clothesline swing
Arcing high,
Soaring, soaring,
Touch the sky.
Tightly holding,
Dreams unfolding,
Further, further,
With each climb.
Ambition realized
The last time.

II

Stillness in the parlor,
Shutters closed real tight,
Everyone is wearing black—
Might as well be night.

Faces set, unsmiling,
Crepe upon the door,
Creepy sort of feeling
Never felt before.

People stand there blinking—
It can't be they're winking—
Coffin's high, nothing shows
Except a wee bit of his nose.

Makes me think of stories
On his lap I heard.
Wish that I could hear him say
Just a single word.

III

Red marble shot and missed.
Blue marble shot and won.
Red marble missed again, again.
Blue marble hit and hit, but then,
Blue marble missed. Too sure, I guess,
Or would it share its happiness?

IV

Winter nights are dark and cold;
Wind is prying, shadows bold.
With each step some warmth retreating,
Eyes quick darting, heart fast beating.
Slow compliance, sense of dread,
Up the staircase and to bed.

V

A shove, a shove;
A punch, a punch.
We stopped speaking
Until lunch.

VI

The battlefield is very green,
The grass is lush and tall.
We aim our broomstick guns and fire,
And charge, retreat, and fall.

We gain the hill, the foe has fled,
We cheer our victory,
Where years before some older boys
Had done the same as we.

And we leave to homeward go,
Did someone back there call?
But no, it's just the wind that blows
The grass that's lush and tall.

VII

Vision lovely,
Pigtailed poise,
Tresses goldspun,
Not like boys.
Disappeared from class one day;
Someone said she'd moved away.

What twelve-year-old
Would be so bold
With others looking on
To ask where she had gone?

Spring

Flowers now are budding,
Twigs are on the trees—
Birds themselves are sunning
In the gentle breeze.

Daylight lasts much longer
Skies appear more blue.
Everyone feels younger
Life seems to start anew.

Bees flit from leaf to petal
Without delay to rest.
Frogs, nightly on their mettle,
Blend solos each with zest.

And so Time turns another page
As Spring breaks forth to view
'Twas ever thus in every age
And yet 'tis ever new.

March 31, 1927

The Letter She Never Received—Chink

The mellow moon of the summer's night
Changed to gold at an instant's sight,
And the glistening waves of the starlit sea
Were dulled when compared to thine eyes of glee,
For those sparkling orbs as they looked into mine
Resembled the luster and brilliance of wine.
The deep-throated laugh which I learned so well
Seemed to be like the chimes of a melodious bell,
While those tousled locks o'er thy Venus-shaped brow
I fancy in mind as I dream of you now
Blown by the winds as the leaves of a tree
Fashioned by nature—a glory to see.
And that same friendly breeze would caressingly stir
To waft through my senses your sweet-scented anguish
The bloom of thy lips and the glow of thy cheeks
Have remained with me still thru' torturous weeks
Stamped in my mind, an indelible print
Your eyes filled with color, your dimples intent.
Ah, my bliss when first we danced arm in arm
For 'twas then I discovered your wondrous charm;
Your sylph-like grace my quickened blood fired
As Helen's proud gaze the Trojan's inspired,
And oft when a blush would spread o'er thy face
I pictured Diane at the head of the Chase.

But enough of good times in memories of yore
Let's look to the future for more in store.
For what is Joy without its sorrow?
Bliss today — a memory tomorrow.
And tho' the time to part has come and gone
I longingly await the Summer's dawn
When once again your smile I'll see
Ah! Elysium! Utopia! Ecstasy!

1928

Memory Lane—Freshman Year

The night Eddie and I were lost ... "Soup" Campbell and the ticket ... Lamont's tales ... Ducky Pond's brother and Albie Booth ... Doremus and Toihalus ... Eddie and the robbery argument ... Swimming ....

MEMORY LANE TO ME

Harry Hartz … the blond nurse … a missing
running board … sixty jokes in the
chorus … Danny reads titles … "throw
up a pillow" … the closet episode …
Flatbush necklace … "The Desert Song"
… water snakes … Weems or Waring …
stuck elevators … the Ventnor theatre …
Ann's sweater idea … broken beads …
a missing stocking … seven in on six
tickets … "Joe's taking a shower" … six
in a canoe … the 1931 party … the knower
… Sea Isle … "Song of the Nile" …
boardwalk benches … three (+) see "Gold
Diggers" … a thorough soaking in a canoe
… Shirley's pun … "The Book of Bette" …
shoes tied under a bed … "Broadway Special" …
wet feet … home late … "Is Notre Dame coed?"
… Dr. Johnson's call … a screen comes out …
Traymore side entrance … Cornel … a sock in
a tree … Joe's mania, "Love Me or Leave Me"
… a squeaky swing … two in a booth …
try and pass Moroney … Charlie's phil-
osophy … the mystery with a string tied
to it … a cute Japanese baby … three tires
… a meal on Pacific Avenue … the
missing turtle … Flatbush customs at 2 A.M.
… "Do you sell Guppy-fish?" … the China-
man joke … and another … cross your
fingers … Ocean City … the Apollo breeze
… the book on bridge by San Luis Rey …

green turns to red ... "The Last of Mrs.
Cheyney" ... feeding the fishes ... books
Ann has read ... antiseptic spilled ...
the chairs at night ... three versions
of the same thing ... the walk through
the bushes ... pretzels ... not rubber,
either ... Cape May ... What I mean!
... lavender ... "Where Is the Song of Songs for Me?"
... the Elks parade ... the ride for dahlias
... and what followed ... "Joe, you're wonderful!" ...
"Did you have a good time yesterday?" ... Cornell
All-American ... Marguerite's coat ...
"The Pagan Love Song" as a floating duet ...
what moonlight sail? ... Harvard men ...
a ripe tomato and an old maid ... a trip
to Brigantine ... the night Joe talked
... "To Be in Love Is Simply Wonderful" ...
a face in a watch ... the Bacchante ...
Ducky's showy ... Marguerite on Stenton
Place ... Gert singing "Moanin' Low" ...
Wildwood ... the Scandels ... "I love it!"
Charlie's memory book ... Lucy for short
... "On a Desert Isle" ... writing on
a strawholder ... wet bathing suits
... a piece of cake ... Question three —
The Big Parade ... Peggy and Ducky ...
three songs put away ... neckpieces
Fred ... the boop-oop-a-doop song ... in
a train especially ... atmospherically
speaking ... Carolina Cops ... out of focus ...

"please?" ... Howard ... a quart on the
thorofare ... Claire ... "give me a ring"
... Alyssina ... No. Philly, in and out ...
mysteries ... the "Smith affair" ... as a
flop ... Dot, to be frank ... died of
heart failure ... Tip ... "Oh, yeah?" ...
"The Single Standard" twice ... dominoes
... alligator pears ... Mr. Smarty ...
mustaches ... Park Pharmacy ... it
rained in the auto ... Junior ... "Let
Me Have My Dreams" ... lipstick ...
hot dog, soda and orange ice ... Pale Moon
... Ventnor Ave. jitney ... fraternity (?)
pin ... Graf Zeppelin, eh, Charlie? ...
"Ain't Misbehavin'" ... Ann's ten (?)
piece bracelet ... wooden heels on the
Boardwalk ... "Ah came heah expecting
a squah deal" ... Ann and the brick-
yard ... in the flesh ... Paramount
Convention ... "Pardon me?" ... several
versions of the same thing ... the 12
o'clock ball ... Joe's life lines ... Lenora's
decision ... several T.L's ....

Summer 1929

Memory Lane to Me

Mrs. Good ... what? more guppies? ... gone
to see a man about a dog ... "Love Me or
Leave Me" ... argumentation ... "You
wouldn't fool me, would you?" ... the
Apollo breeze ... luscious roadster ... "Where
the — are those tennis balls?" ... "Splendor
of God" ... a newspaper clipping ... "My
Song of the Nile" ... "Died for dear old
Rutgers" ... "The better to see you with,
my dear" ... Mr. McDonough ... and
what he said, Gertrude ... gumparking
... songs to fill up space ... Sez you ...
my curiosity ... Parlor Car No. 18 ...
two seats in the aisle ... "Can't We Be
Friends?" ... "Can't You Understand?" ...
a baseball game last Easter ... "You don't
look tootle-oo" ... "The newspaper is a
day late now" ... Christmas holidays
... stuck in Pittsburgh ... "Is Mr. Fran-
cis Hewitt there?" ... the Stevens ...
"Show of Shows" ... "You know my
uncle" ... a long walk, and the
longest bull session on record ...
complexes ... memories ... "If I Had
a Talking Picture of You" ... "Aren't We
All" ... B. S. ... Squab ... Absence Makes
The Heart Grow Fonder ... ribs ... two
undertakers ... a letter at Xmas ...
Western Sandwich ... green lipstick ...
read a thousand times ... "Condemned"

... Betchens ... Gablo ... just like one big
happy family ... cinnamon on toast ...
balloons ... what advice in the auto? ...
stood up — Margie? ... "Devil May Care" ...
waltzing as such ... "To ——— " ...
complications ... and circumlocutions ...
tipping hats ... widows ... "Our Mutual
Friend" ... green grass ... and "I've got to
go home" ... "Does this road lead to
the White Horse Pike?" ... Caracas and
Curaçao ... "Without Love" ... ice cream and
watching the car ... "You're holding out on me"
... charms and watch-chains ... "Joe's
a wise guy" ... a single pair of mice ...
Charlie's hat ... "I hope you find the door"
complexes again ... "Exactly Like You"
... just one more trial ... is it a bet?
... "After the Ball" ....

Winter 1929 to 1930

Memory Lane — Sophomore Year

We chose a fire ... Why did Elmer leave
Lefferts? ... Lexington Arms, and danger!
... The Brooklyn witches' mystery ...
Elmer and Grace L., or wasn't it Grace? ...
The old gym and the night it burned ...
Harlan Stiff ... and H.S.M. Herd ...
The robbery ....

What Two Years in College Taught Me

1. That college doesn't fit me for anything.

2. That swearing isn't inexcusable.

3. That the less seriously one can take life, the better.

4. That college profs actually are absent-minded, but aren't infallible.

5. That bull sessions are vastly more educational than most courses.

6. That fraternities and girls don't mix with studies.

7. That there is literature more interesting than fiction.

8. That there is a lot of good in everyone.

9. That college men drink solely to show off.

10. That life is a hell of a mess.

11. That the average college fellow is ignorant, and willing to remain so—as long as he may have his good time.

Memory Lane—Summer 1930

"Until the End"... lollipops and gumdrops...
"We'll be back later"... disappointment...
She turned her back! ... transgressing again
... the reverse side of a record ..."How's busi-
ness you liar?!"... Omf ..."You've Got That Thing"
and "You Do Something to Me"... who-who...
more milk wagons and third floors ... my
gold tennis ball ... oh, for a few minutes ...
the mystery of the lone guppy ... lightning
never strikes twice ... blasé changes ...
cheerio ... reincarnation ..."Chili Girl"...
worse than Joe ..."Do You Play, Young Man?"...
a Brigantine thunderstorm ... a lift ...
"How do you feel, Doris?"... five skates ...
Dreams are best ..."Recaptured Love" via
Brigantine ..."Have a hardboiled egg? ...
"Around the Corner"... Cronikers ... have you
any pretzels ... who said ginger ale ...
3 A.M. ... fifteen minutes to make a train
..."Way Out West"..."My Future Just Past"
... and what did ... Full moon, but no sail ...
wooden spoons ... Margie's last night ...
Joe and the Bulletins ... Coca-Cola's, in the
same store ... Black and White ... Pale Moon
... 4,000 beds ... the palmist, and what
she said about crowds ..."Home for Wayward
Girls"... shoot-the-shoots ... Sea Gate
Cops ... How many gin-rickies does it
take at 35¢ each? ... and a cop ...
Boogey, boogey-boo ... Don't be a bobo ...

feel punchy ... a moment in a hall ... Fair and Warmer ... We like you, Charlie ... "Bye Bye Blues" ... Just a Little Closer ... the last night, and a bus ride ... "Holiday" ... Thought anything subtle, Joe? ... "Three Little Sisters" ... Charlie and the dead aviator ... It's a boat-race and the boat's full of Chinks ... Leggetts and a soda ... West Africa ... Doris asks a favor ... "The Dawn Patrol" ... Journey's End ... ... drying dishes ....

Memory Lane—Junior Year

Hiram Street phone calls … Hot-cha-cha
… the "Rutgers night" at the Uproar …
the drunk from Washington State …
Middletown, New York … and the welcome! …
"Watch me walk this straight line" …
"the Bettys" … what Prof. Crow heard on
the stairs … Weston Mills, first time …
Steve's broken arm … Rosie and the Polock
… Colored Baptist Church … the all-night
bridge session … Drs. Boyden … and the
petition to Dean Partch … Dr. Cole …
Deer Park … Shelter Island and God's
Country … "Horsey" Marvin … calculus in
one minute! … Non-Euclidian Geometry
… Archie the star witness … the last
ferry … Christmas Mystery … Dale
Roberts and Bach … Everett Key and Helen
… synthetic gin … George MacDon-
ald snipe hunting … Ozzie Nelson and
New York … Measley vs. Garon in Lakewood
… "Birdy" Beaks … "the wild piney
flavor" … "Here is no megalomaniacal
schizophrenic" … "the smack and
tang of element things" ….

After Three College Years I Find

1. That nothing matters except one's mental attitude.

2. That smoking is beneficial, for a number of reasons.

3. That college men drink for any number of reasons, and not just to show off.

4. That jealousy is the basis of most wrong.

5. That Joe's philosophy — getting the most enjoyment out of each moment — is sound.

6. That sharing one's burden lightens one's own.

Memory Lane — Summer 1931

"It's smart to be thrifty"... Charlie almost
pinched ... busted windshield ... My
Pal ... "Sweet and Lovely"... Waltzing
and driving ... "Too bad you couldn't make
the team"... Atlantic City Casino ... "It's in
the pot"... Ozzie Nelson ... Joe's sweater
... My sweater! ... "Free for All"...
Psychoanalysis ... Marj O'Neill ... "Minnie
had a heart as big as a whale"... Joe and the
canary bird ... Joe and the punch-board ...
five minutes of continuous playing ...
two matches — relax! ... "I Just Can't
Write the Words"... "The Lady of My Dreams"
... no orchestra, no eats ... "Tiger Rag"
... No sun, no stars ... molasses ...
The girl with the red slippers ... blowout
in Ocean City ... Charlie's clothes ...
onions tonight ... a banana ... Father
Heille and the "Vampire"... the long-postponed
date ... "He's girl crazy"... Avenue I milk-
men ... July mornings ... An Ocean
City window ... Botfields ... "Mr. Bozo
to you"... Pepper in ginger ale ... layer
cake ... stones in the ears ... Lake Lenape
... Spanish custom ... Mrs. S. and the
rumble ... "As silver as silver can be"... "Of
Human Bondage"... Lawless girls ...
Joe's last night ... "Risque" revelations

…"Come back later when the proprietor is here"… Hotel Astor, Trenton … three football games …"There's a tree in back of you"… More blood spilt, in Brooklyn ….

Memory Lane — Senior Year

Grandpa ... Scarlet sock ... "We're just like ions" ... Susie ... the midgets ... that's the truth ... "Maybe" ... ice skates needed ... Pat ... no water, no gas ... "Me —" ... "Clara, Lou, and M" ... Tom Porter and Mickey Walker ... the rabbit that ran between Earl's legs ... football under a piano ... Zeke's approach forcing system ... Art and the Jack of Hearts ... short-sheeted ... the drinking contest ... "Harpo" Weinhagen ... "Moanin' Low" Garon ... Moe Hamelsky ... Ross and the keys ... the red-headed nurse ... Winham at Yale — or was it Wellesley? ... Mt. Holyoke x 34 ... Porter's Million Dollar Baby ... Larry Leeds at sea ... Is my face red? ... Not Dr. Whitman's son! ... Ratings ... "Petting Patty" ... Guy Lombardo ... the bells must ring! ... searchlight on the roof ... drunk again Conover ... the midnight lunch ... Phil and his Auburn ... "You have a spiritual look" ... the Bradley Studio salesman ... I'm a physical ed. student ... Mutual Circulation Co ... Ruth Penthouse ... Virtuous V ... Newark and the Love Bird ... Lake Garrett ... through the Coop in blankets ... the picture Harry will never know ... Richard the Roue ... "Two diamonds and I don't mean your eyes" ... "You've changed" ... Jobinus ... "What Price

College?"... How to do it, No 2 ... Steve and I walk ... Smith vs. the H.S. Sweetheart ... letters from the dead ... Pat and her grandmother ... Tom's stomach ... Dapper Dick the Hapless Hadden ... Bill Owen in India ... Dorothy Fullerton ... Wilbur and I at Weston Mills ..."The Thrill Is Gone"..."Red Wing"... malignant jitters ... Heinie Benkert ... Joe Miller laughs and I ..."the boy Conover"... Discussing Socrates with Cris, the Turkish waiter, over pancakes and coffee at 2 A.M.... Buck, Earl, and I are ostracized ..."A very high 2, Mr. Hewitt"..."My Star: a fine girl"... Hangover Harry: Fruit ... Whitman's brief case ..."My God! Where's the Phi Joke key?"..."Congratulations, Mr. Metzgar!"... Jonie ..."My life is a closed book"..."Pardon me, but would you two care to ride in the rumble seat?"... Desecrates, the Greek philosopher ..."Wring your neck, or just neck?"..."April Fool, I hope you bite"..."And with this, Mr. Hewitt, we bid you a fond farewell"... Dot and Irene ... Elmer's sudden departure ... Harry's 1 in Poetry ... Earl and the photostatic copy ... the New York Library ..."O.K. Czecho-Slovakia"... Buck and I in the dumps during exams ... Cut plug: Harry and I ... Ross ... the Civil War Bull Sessions ... listening in the dark ... Bob

Schneider as Mata Hari ... Lehigh in a rumble ... the picture contest ... the Anthologist jokes ... "the slipping of silken buttons thru the woolen underwear of time" ... hoot like an owl ... "Am I right? Of course I am!" ... Is Art for Art's sake a matter of temperament or intellect? ... Yes, professor ... "Daddy will, but Mother won't let me" ... "I'll invite you" ... See that 'Behind!' ... "Epic Visions of the World" by Houston Peterson ... Is the night dark and chilly ... "I have been faithful to thee, Cynara" ... "Je ne sais quois" ... the Three Ayes Men ... repetitions ... "A kiss! when all is said —" ... "Shelley is a beautiful but ineffectual angel—" ... Laureate of Love ... locked out at Xmas ... Belford's goat ... Junior Prom ... Ross, I, and the "Sex Factor" ... Hoohoo Harry ... all their grist is mill ... a peach of a pair ... "Where sportive ladies leave their doors ajar" ... do you want a whole exposure ... mousing out ... The Woodbridge Dance—and what followed ... "After all, we're only novitiates, you know" ... Harry calls up Fords ... Deener Vogele ... Luzmela ... Buck and I and two cigars ... the Commencement parade ... the bee at Graduation ... ... studying for the poetry quiz (?) ... Geneva Inn and Harry's car ....

After Four College Years It Seems

1. That college broadens the mind and gives one a finer sense of values.

2. That cynicism and introspection are the grave by-products of education.

3. That the simple life may be better after all.

4. That much of what one learns in college one forgets—thank God!

Homecoming

You sing to yourself, your heart beats so fast
No wonder, my lad, for you're home at last.
Back home from afar, with its warmth and cheer—
Back to old haunts until the new year.
You see the old place looming there up ahead
And you picture your room with its rickety bed.
So you reach the gate—to the house in no time
And though needless to tell you, it's a feeling sublime
To see your old ma standing there at the door
And know it's just you she's waiting there for;
To fall in her arms with a laugh and a sigh
And hide that wet blur that comes over your eye;
To hug her and kiss her and squeeze her so tight
While she's thanking God you got home all right.
Then behind her's your dad, the finest that's made—
A little more worn, a trifle bit grayed,
One arm round your shoulder, his hand in your own
Renewing at once, the understanding you've known
From the earliest times when as comrades you took
Long walks together through the woods 'cross the brook.

I tell you, my lad, it's a wonderful thing
To think that happiness with you you'll bring
To those folks hanging on your every word
Just worshipping you—gee, ain't it absurd?
For then you think of the days gone before
When you neglected your ma, and resolve that no more
You'll spend your first night with the blond 'cross the way.
Or go off with the boys on the following day.
Sure, take your old sweetheart where she wants to go

And with your old buddy enjoy a good show—
But make that one sweetheart your dear little old ma
And as for your buddy—take the best of them—pa:
For no matter how sweet the girlfriend may be
Or how fine the boys, I'm sure that you'll see
That the ones who have loved you from the day of your birth
Are the ones you most cherish of all on the earth.
So, love them, respect them, and show them the way
You'd like your own son to treat you some day.

December 17, 1929

Summer's End

Just a few sheets of paper clasped loosely together—
    A record of joys that were yours and mine;
A symbol of all we'll remember forever
    When we think of the Summer of Twenty-nine.

December 25, 1929

The Parting

Whoso would be joyful let him!
There's no surety for the morrow.

—Lorenzo dé Medici

It seemed as though when Summer ended
All our happiness was past—
But even in those days so splendid
We sort of knew it couldn't last.

For when the day to part drew near
Our plans lost all their zest,
A stifled sigh, a tell-tale tear
Betrayed a leadened breast.

But to the end our laughter rang—
Smiles tried to conquer fears,
Though that last night, those songs we sang,
The words were blurred by tears.

We aimed to hide in gayest guise
Those pangs from parents dear,
And they in turn wiped moistened eyes,
Sad mem'ry in a tear.

For they, I fear, recalled the day
Of another parting when
Each one was cheered upon his way
To never meet again.

But that was not the way to feel,
We knew it and we played the game.
Though sadness tried to oft reveal
Its presence, we sang on the same.

No, I'll wager that 'twas rare
A clouded brow you saw appear;
Though now and then a vacant stare
Betokened thought of parting near.

It sure was hard to see them leave—
For well we knew each breast concealed
An aching heart resigned to grieve
As sadness in each face revealed.

And now our crowd has gone the way
So many others have before;
Let's hope we'll meet again some day
To join in pleasure as of yore.

Oh, would that I could see them now:
To hear again Dan's soothing voice,
Or spend what time I could allow
To search Joe's words for double choice.

To make one little girl deplore
That Greta ever was a name;
Or laugh at Marion's jokes once more
And think, "Poor girl, she's not to blame."

To see again Ann's cheery face,
Or envy Mike his languid air;
To find in Gert that pleasing grace,
Or Charlie's comradeship but share.

Oh, would the fates those times repeat
And make it Summer, just for a day,
So that their friends each one might meet—
Yes, just for once, then come what may.

To spend one night beneath the moon—
Let fact and fancy mingle free;
To gaily sing, or softly croon
Those songs of treasured memory.

The Past

Let me linger over the memory of
scenes which have passed away.

—Plato

No doubt you've had the feeling, too,
As though the Summer's fled too fast;
You're cheated, saddened, wistful, blue,
Existing daily in the past?

You silly thing! That's not the way,
Don't sigh and gaze so mournfully;
Though it may hurt, just smile, be gay—
No sense regretting what must be.

So come and picture now with me
Those glorious times of days gone by,
Let's wander now through memory,
I'll help you, please—come on, just try.

You'll find a chuckle in each rhyme,
At times a subtle meaning, too;
Mayhap some deed which at the time
Though hidden, we all knew.

Sure, you recall the picture show
That night we took in at the Strand,
When seven went where six should do
Beyond the gateman's hand?

One day stands out in silhouette:
A picnic crowd without a care,
When Charlie got us soaking wet,
Though playful Ann did all her share!

In Ocean City we came to look
For medals in Joe's tennis play;
Though once the only roads we took—
Running boards were scarce that day!

Recall the night Joe cracked the joke:
"Here comes the Big Parade, I see."
And how unconsciously she spoke,
"Did I hear someone speak of me?"

Again we sat upon the beach
And saw—my gosh! could my eyes err?
Someone walking with a peach—
Say, Charlie, care for lavender?

A girl and boy had mysteries
That each would solve the while;
The one besought "Apollo's breeze,"
The other found a "Desert Isle."

Songs in Summer had their share,
"The Pagan's Love" we thought divine,
Especially when as a pair
Two sang while floating in the brine.

The "Desert Song," though not the tune—
Will make two laugh, though why, untold;
While "Moanin' Low" (how she could croon!)
Made more than one grow "hot" from cold!

Boardwalk benches once held sway
In what the well-dressed youth should do.
Why, even pretzels had their day—
Though one I'm still afraid to chew.

Oh, I could mention many things
I'm sure'd provoke your memory—
To Flatbush beads my thought still clings,
And Harry Hartz and Question Three.

Deep night ... Pale Moon ... swing to and fro
(Be still there, Tip, you noisy pup);
Or what we'd really like to know,
Did Lucy throw the pillow up?

Or just what Danny slipped and said
That night when bookstores were the vogue;
Or what the Cornel "sipper" read—
No, Dan, you weren't the only rogue.

Those hidden chuckles we enjoyed
For thoughtless words were far from few,
Bacchante's name makes one annoyed
And Stenton Place is taboo, too.

So now, you see, that mournful mood
Has vanished from your face;
Mayhap these verses have seemed crude
But smiles have found their place.

And you will find a smile soon paves
The shortest path to happiness,
While side by side, as willing slaves
Walk your ideals, assured success.

The Crowd

All who joy would win
Must share it. Happiness was born a twin.

—Byron

Why, here they are, through mem'ry's charm,
The whole dear crowd, engrossed in talk,
Laughing gaily, as arm in arm,
They idly wander down the walk ...

Dan

Who is that upon the end?
Don't tell me that you cannot guess!
Though mustache to his features lend
More charm, it's Danny, nonetheless.

How firm the saunter of his stride—
His hands behind his back;
How strong his friendship, often tried
And never found by test to lack.

Such full contagious laughs had he
That to our own they often led;
And when embarrassed one might see
His burning blush of violent red.

His counsels wise we realized
Were worthy of our thought;
His commendation highly prized
For 'twas less found than sought.

Ann

But who so dainty next in line
Between those two chaps, Joe and Dan?
With sturdy stride and charm divine—
Well, who of course, but our dear Ann.

Little Ann—I see her, still,
The kind of girl you'd want to meet.
One glance from her—oh, what a thrill!
Makes hearts thought cold skip up a beat.

A curly blond, as I recall,
With ruddy cheeks and healthy eyes,
Quite cute and plump, not very tall—
The type that causes long-drawn sighs.

With her you must be on your toes—
Your jokes must be right off the press,
For she, you see, attends the shows,
I've said enough, the rest you guess.

Joe

And then, as I have said, comes Joe—
Though thoughts fly fast, what shall I say?
Who can describe that pleasing glow
Of comradeship he proved each day?

Who best can find beneath his mask
Of cheer in days of dark despair
An aching heart whose burdened task
Concealed from all its double care?

Ah, yes, you say he's full of fun
But more than half you've left untold,
For 'neath that tendency to pun
You'll find a friend of richest gold.

No fear to find him wanting when
You need a pal to see you through,
If ever he's your pal, 'tis then,
God bless you, Joe, for you're true blue.

Ducky

A stately figure's next in line
With quiet grace and charming air,
A regal head with features fine,
Bewitching eyes of luster rare.

Yes, it's Ducky, devastating;
The ideal model for your queen.
Scintillating, fascinating,
So captivating. What I mean!

Infrequently at best you'll find
A girl so versatile as she,
For rarely beauty's found combined
With charming personality.

The kind of girl enshrined in dreams—
The sunshine of the rainy day;
Each word I write the less it seems
I mention half I meant to say.

CHARLIE

A tall bronzed youth with curly hair
I single out whom you must know;
It's Charlie, wistful, debonair,
Amusing, grave, vivacious, slow.

A strange admixture, this you'll see
That few possess and none but he
Could blend in noble harmony
Such contrasts shaded to agree.

A prince of chaps, I'll have you know,
Too quick to lend a helping hand;
The kind to whom you always go
Because you know he'll understand.

I wish I had the gifted way
To tell you all he seems to me,
But space is short, suffice to say,
He's just what I would like to be.

MARGUERITE

And next in line is Marguerite,
'Tis odd the rhymes some names conjure:
So apropos—petite and sweet,
Or better still, demure and pure.

Her own good times she sacrificed
So thoughtful was she of the rest,
Mayhap it was she realized
Our joy made her the happiest.

Benign contentment always spread
Where e're her dainty footsteps strayed;
Her sympathetic manner led
To counsel her when needing aid.

You doubt that such a fine array
Can in one person scarcely be?
Just know her brothers and you'll say
It runs in all the family.

Mike

Then, Michael's unaffected pose
Betrays his easy-going way,
While at his mouth a Murad glows
And smoky rings about him play.

But do not this way be misled
And think him heedless of the rest,
For his demeanor shields instead
The kindest acts he made his quest.

At times before we voiced a need
He volunteered to help us out,
Sometimes a word, more oft a deed,
Removed an obstacle of doubt.

A little shy, and hardly gay,
His subtle puns we caught through tone.
His, a quiet, modest way
That made our Michael all our own.

And though it may seem odd to you
I must mention one thing more:
A dainty package, small, 'tis true,
That Gert brought with her to the shore.

'Twas little seen but nonetheless
We felt a pang when it must go.
What package? Can't you even guess?
Why I mean Lucy, now you know.

Some others, too, I can't forget
For each means something to our past;
Though short their stay, to our regret,
They made strong friendships, long to last.

The first of all, I mention Claire,
I wish that we had seen her more.
Mayhap some day her presence fair
Will grace our shore like days of yore.

Then Doris bobs into my mind
Such is the charm of memory,
A good time one was sure to find
When you were in her company.

And Marion's midnight twinkling eyes
Betray her tendency for fun
Though few may in her realize
That deeper, finer channels run.

Veronica, I left to last
Because she sort of seemed to me
A symbol of a vanished past
Portraying what again may be.

For there were days you can't forget
Before our crowd e're came to be
When each of us a different set
Belonged to with our loyalty.

But where are they, I ask you, now,
Those friendly groups of days of yore?
You meet by chance? a passing bow—
A few small words, but nothing more.

You say that this can never be
That ties unite us far too strong?
I pray you're right, that we will see
Our crowd together through years long.

The Future

He lives who has lived.

—Machado

But gee! We did have wondrous times—
I glory in their pleasures still,
They seem to stand out in my mind
Impressions made that years can't fill.

So when you're feeling sort of blue
And times drag by when things go wrong—
Why, if you've nothing else to do
Read this again, it won't take long.

You'd be surprised how comforting
Are all the mem'ries that it stirs,
To hear once more the laughter ring
And feel the joy that naught deters.

To picture each in mind again
Whose different paths brought but regret,
To sort of make you wistful when
It brings back thoughts you can't forget.

I hope you won't be feeling bad
For that is what I would destroy.
Remember this: each thought so sad
Is but reflected from some joy.

And that those others, just as you
Have memories of days of yore,
So try to plan, as they plan too
For future days of joy in store.

And now it's time that I should close
For my delightful task is done,
Depicted are the scenes that rose
In mind from distant Summer's fun.

I've tried to tell as best I might
Just what I thought of each of you—
Sincere and frank, I hope not trite,
Impressions gleaned from things I knew.

The dedication of this tale
I've left until the last—
To you, dear friends, who never fail
I wrote this story of the past.

To you, I think it needless to
Apologize for mismade rhymes
For I've but tried to bring anew
The happiness of other times.

For you will find where e're you go
In search of what you call success
The wisest men are those who know
Life's greatest gift is happiness.

So now, dear friends, I say good-bye,
Or better still an au revoir,
For each of you, I hope, will try
To help our crowd unite once more.

To make the past a living thing
Which shifting sands cannot erase
As each new spring its joys may bring
To strengthen ties that years efface.

So will you each keep close in mind
This little cycle I repeat,
For in it you may often find
That with a smile your cares you greet.

Another Spring? a joy to be,
Another Summer? ecstasy,
Another Fall? farewell's decree,
A Winter long? sweet memory.

And if the Fates direct us far
Upon the stream of Life's vast sea,
We'll know, each one — where e're we are —
I'll think of you, you'll think of me.

For thus it is, you'll see some day,
That wealth is measured, not in gold,
But in those treasures of the mind,
Those cherished mem'ries, hallowed — old.

You'll find new friendships as you stride
Along Life's winding way,
But now and then, your thoughts will glide
To those of yesterday.

For though they're buried deep, you'll see
Those youthful friendships stood the test;
No matter what the rest may be—
The friends of youth you'll love the best.

OUTRACE THE DAWN

From 1930 to 1933

Hours

The hours resemble people that one meets,
Some shunned, endured but for convention's sake,
And others like a brother whom one greets
To tie anew the bonds no years can break.
At work, they hurry by unrecognized,
As street crowds jostle as they pass;
Alone, they linger as though hypnotized,
To strain the patience of the hourglass.

But hours with you are like a host of friends,
So various, so sweet with new delight,
So timeless that their presence never ends
But fills the lonely chambers of the night.

And when we two the stairs of mem'ry climb,
Hours cling like kisses to the lips of time.

January 9, 1930

Reproach

Perhaps I should have stiffly stood
When first our trails crossed in that wood
        And let you pass as silently
As you yourself, for tho' I spoke
But dumb response the echoes broke ...
        You might at least have noticed me.

And when we met the formal way
Some condescension bid you say
        A stilted phrase of greeting—we
Whom well you knew had met one day
Tho' not in this, the usual way ...
        You might at least have smiled at me.

I came to know your manner proud
And for your whims, I think, allowed.
        But fool I was, I could not see
That others baited, snared as I
Were cast aside without a sigh ...
        You did not have to play with me.

And then you spurned me like the rest
And tho' your fickleness I guessed
        You did not even tell me why.
But still I love you now as then
And since we'll never meet again
        You might at least have said goodbye.

January 9, 1930

To ———

When the sun hides its face in the glow of the West
And each cloud is bedecked in magnificent hue
Then the memories surge through my lonely lead breast
And I think of a day long ago spent with you.

When we sat by the side of a shimmering lake
Far away from the strife of the world—just we two—
In a spot that is hallowed for memories' sake,
A remembrance I'll cherish forever. Will you?

Where a soft lang'rous breeze swayed the strands of your hair
And the tint of the lake graced your eyes of pale blue
While the light of the sun flushed your features so fair:
It's no wonder I think of that one day with you.

And 'twas there, side by side, our opinions we aired
As in happiness' quest we pursued but a clue
Seeking blindly afar what we thoughtlessly shared
At that moment when I was together with you.

Oh, it isn't the sky, and it isn't the sun
And it isn't the path to the spot that we knew—
It's an infinite something not easily won
That brought happiness to me that moment with you.

And it may be that sometime when you've gone away
I'll return to that spot to seek comfort anew
In the happiness felt in my soul to this day
To recall that contentment I found there with you.

Or perchance it may be that 'tis I who must part
And that you may be led to the lake in my lieu.
Oh! 'tis then I pray God that the pain leave your heart
When through memories' charm I will sit there with you.

January 9, 1930

Pals

There is something that's finer than friendship,
It's a feeling that's deeper than love, —
A sublime sort of thing in your heart's-grip
That is God's greatest gift from Above.

It's a confidence in a pal when
There might be room for some doubt;
And understanding between two men
That women know nothing about.

It's giving and taking in all things
Without bother to balance accounts;
It's soothing your buddy's worst heart stings
And cheering him to the last ounce.

It's fighting his battles if need be
And sharing the credit you won;
It's helping him some way he can't see
Then forgetting what you have done.

It's not talking much about friendship
But it's giving him all you have got
And when he does wrong or makes some slip
Then it's sharing his stigma or blot.

For there comes in the lives of all, I fear, —
The time a girl's comfort won't do—
And I'm hoping that I will always be near
To do all I can to help you.

January 28, 1930

The Diary

Best be to cast aside your book
        With memories recorded there.
For in its covers ev'ry look
        Will plunge like knives in breast laid bare.

Each page thus turned will bring anew
        Those youthful days beyond recall—
But not the happy times you knew;
        Just painful mem'ries, that is all.

A joyous night, a moment's bliss
        Brought back as gifts from Heaven sent—
The thrill ecstatic of a kiss
        Repaid with reminiscent dread torment.

Those pleasures are not lightly won,
        And dreams outweigh the joys you took,
Live for today, let past be done:
        Best be to cast aside your book.

February 13, 1930

Fame

Deter your heedless haste to Fame—
    That fruitless chase, that pursuit blind;
    No matter what may be your aim
'Tis some creation of the mind
Which once attained will not appease
    Your thirst, yet rather lend it fire,
    And thus your passion less relieve
Than heighten such a false desire;

For Fame is like to Happiness,
    That never is, but always sought—
    The end achieved, 'tis dead success:
Idealization razed to nought.
Best be to strive for mortal things:
    Accomplishment brings peace and rest
    Than trust to fruitless hammerings
At Glory's lockless door you quest.

For though some insight might expose
    The way to Fame behind that door,
    Yet entrance e'en to him who knows
Is gained by costly pay before:
For all who enter forfeit here
    Friendship and Love—Fame's price well paid
    And live in sorrow and in fear
Repeating long the bargain made.

February 20, 1930

Lost Love

I always thought I loved you so
With all your fickle subtle ways,
And even thought my love would grow
To cherish you through all my days.
I dreamed that you were born divine—
A creature fashioned just for me,
To guard and fondle and be mine
E'en to, at last, eternity.

But now I know you for your worth
Through disillusion's bitter eyes;
Thou child of Hell's own mortal earth
I've seen behind your gay disguise.
You were but formed to break my heart—
To ferment sorrow, pain, and strife;
Best be for me that soon we part:
You are not worth the struggle—Life.

June 15, 1930

Driftwood

Little bits of driftwood, playthings of the waves
Bound to vagrant wand'ring, to the winds but slaves;
Careless of their destiny, common fates they share
Tossed to rest they know not why, or when, or even where.

Human bits of driftwood, hurtled on through life,
Broken by its pounding, everlasting strife;
Hapless in its grasping tides, borne on currents slight
Washed to rest on shoreless seas of eternal night.

June 28, 1930

A Lost Chum

Somehow the days seem duller
Our plans have lost their zest;
Somehow the world's lost color
Since our old chum went West.

Somehow he was a master of men—
He was the one who led.
Somehow it didn't seem possible when
We were told that he was dead.

Somehow we know he's quite as near
As if he'd never gone away;
Somehow he fills us still with cheer
Lighting the path along our way.

Autumn

Green leaves are turning grayish brown,
Then at leisure come tumbling down.
Fleecy clouds, once white and bright,
Seem much darker overnight.
Ocean billows rise on high
As the days go slipping by.
Twilight deepens into gloom;
Roses quick to lose their bloom.
Wingéd creatures, fast in flight
Travel south at some great height.
The red sun, though slow to admit defeat,
Is no more oppressive with his heat.
Foliage demurring to give in, too
Finally relinquishes its emerald hue.
So Autumn enters with this debut,
As Summer bids us fond adieu.

De Profundis — A Sonnet

When weary sun is pillowed in the west
And anxious friends are grouped about my bed,
Straining their ears to heed a last request
Before I seek companions in the dead,
I shall thank them all, grateful for their aid,
Take each one by hand, make a last reply,
And quietly, all preparations made,
I shall close my eyes and smiling, — die.

Then they will shake their heads and say,
"Tis strange that he should dying, smile this way.
Life and love were joys to him unknown,
He trod a weary hermit trail alone."

But one in memory will cry awhile,
And musing, hear their words, know why I smile.

Elysium

Did you ever wish for a quiet spot
To dream of bye-gone days?
To clear from your memory Time's great blot
And remove from your mind Life's maze?

Did you ever wish to fly away
From the city's bustle and strife
To a forest deep in which to stray
And pass the rest of your life?

Did you ever wish to be high in the hills
Alone by a ramblin' stream
Away from one's cares and woes and ills —
Just to sit by that brook and dream?

Did you ever wish to go down to the sea
In the ships that go sailing by …
If you have, you've got my sympathy
For you've the same feeling as I.

Embers

Strange that the flame still flickers in the grate
Despite neglect that saw it fade unfed.
I wonder now, —is it not yet too late—
To fan the spark, or let it pass for dead?
"Despite neglect?" Ah, no, despite the fear,
Despite the devils dancing on the pyre,
Dancing red and green, dancing in a tear,
Dancing like puppets on a heart-strung wire.
A breath will kill the spark, will ease the pain
And leave a mark that none will ever know;
A sigh will fan the flame to writhe again
In an ecstatic bitter-sweetened glow.
To sigh, and cause the flame to burn anew?
Or breathe, and breathing die? I wish I knew.

DREAM CASTLES

A moment free I found the chance
To seek a lonely solitude—
Away from laughter, music, dance,
Where I thought none would there intrude.

I found my music in the sea
My partners were my dreams set free
To strain at hopes and reverie;
The dance was that of Life to me.

I built my castle in the air
And fenced it with enchanted charms
And ruled it with my Queen so fair
Who danced e'en then in others' arms.

'Twas easy thus to plan and scheme
And build my fortress—I confess;
To love is nothing but to dream
Forever seeking happiness.

For dreams though built upon the sand
Are steadfast through the wildest strife
Where actions fail, ideals still stand
And pave with peace the path of Life.

What cared I then for earthly ways?
A thousand woes? a rival's fame?
I had but to avert my gaze
And each would fade an empty name.

In that rapt mood I wandered wild,
And planned for days in years to be—
My jealousy her charms beguiled
Though I knew they were not for me.

How long I stood I cannot guess
Until they missed me from the floor
And though I danced, yet, nonetheless
I whirled in dreams e'en as before.

For when I saw her face by chance
Alit with pleasure's carefree zest,
Scarce noticing my ardent glance—
I realized then that dreams are best.

In them love's castles cannot fall
And in the overladen breast—
Through disillusion's bitter pall
I saw anew that dreams are best.

July 8, 1930

We Little Know

We little know what years will bring—
What sorrow and distress;
We think of but today and sing
Deceived in happiness.

We little know the secret joy
We cherish will decay;
The wanton years too soon destroy
What best we love today.

We little know what love's dreams are,
They change and fade from day to day;
We hitch our wagons to a star
But find ideals are crumbling clay.

We little know the hopes and fears
Concealed within each breast,
Nor could we stop the flood of tears
E'en though their cause we guessed.

We little know each time we part
If e'er we'll meet the while,
And if a sobbing broken heart
Is hidden 'neath each smile.

We little know if each good-bye
Will be our very last—
How soon we each of us may die
And all our woes be past.

We little know who are our friends,
    What breasts conceal that sacred glow
Which steadfast burns until all ends
    We little know ... We little know.

July 18, 1930

The Sun and Moon

Slowly the sun has traced its way
    Across the western sky,
Foretold by shadows ends the day
    And thus the sunbeams die.

Slowly my sun has traced its way—
    Now low that once was high,
And as I sink to rest, I pray,
    And then like sunbeams, die.

Slowly the moon has risen high
    To bathe the Earth below
With its effulgence from the sky,
    Contentment in its glow.

Holy—my soul may quickly rise;
    Forgot is earthly strife—
With God's Communion in the skies
    I find a better life.

July 28, 1930

Questions

Why must this turmoil rack my mind
And fill my heart with doubt and fear?
Where may I sweet contentment find
In friendship's always open ear?

Why must the world be filled with those
Whose selfish deeds but foster pain?
Whose jealous nature slowly grows
And blots out friends through Envy's stain?

Why do those friends I most hold dear
Mistake my actions at each turn? . . .
Dare I but hope one single tear
Is hidden 'neath their censure stern?

Why must regret stand uppermost
In every thought and vagrant dream?
While memory — that haunting ghost —
In writhing torture reigns supreme.

Why do so few of those remain
Of whom I once could call a friend?
Will some with me that bond retain
Steadfast in heart until the end?

Will I some day my hopes confess
    To one whose charm is ever new?
Will that someone find happiness?
    And will I find mine that day, too?

August 3, 1930

Three Days

Blindly I groped through bitter strife—
Pierced by regret, keen as a knife—
Praying for peace, the end of life...
But that was Yesterday.

Spoken a word and skies are clear—
Laughter and joy drying each tear—
Steadfast the bond we each hold dear...
And that is Today.

Down Life's river both our ways wend
Seeking the secret beyond the bend—
Paddling together, friends till the end...
But that is Tomorrow.

August 4, 1930

Escape

As Cressid lay within her tent
And waited for her love to come,
Unmindful of the closing doom
On all the souls in Ilium;

As he who at a Concord pond
Retreated to bucolic thought,
While all about life's social bonds
That chained the rest grew taut;

So, while men shout in wild alarm
And struggle blindly for the light,
I lay me on a grassy mound
And envy soaring birds in flight.

AGAIN

Again the summer days are nigh,
Those days so precious yesteryear—
Each one on which we built
Our hopes, but not without some fear.

Again the sun shines in the sky
On each of those we held so dear,
But now the laughter in the eye
Is hidden by a wistful tear.

Again we meet the same as yore—
"The same?" —I wonder if it be?
Have we the love e'en as before—
Or is it cherished memory?

Again another crowd has passed
The way all crowds must someday go:
We hoped, we dreamed that ours would last
Yet knew it couldn't long be so.

Again those older heads nod wise:
They knew just how 'twould end the while
They see forgotten faces rise
And hide their sorrow with a smile.

Again let's sing in manner gay
No sense to mourn for what must be,
If one must think of yesterday
Make it a joyous memory.

August 9, 1930

Last Night I Dreamed

Last night I dreamed a wondrous dream: —
　　A star-sown night on gliding tide
Canoeing down a moonlit stream —
　　And you were seated at my side.

It seemed so real, a life's desire
　　Wrapped in a moment's paradise,
A burning hope with love's hot fire
　　An instant mine to realize.

I dreamed your lips met mine to kiss,
　　Yet parted with Fate's sudden fears;
Then when I woke from slumb'rous bliss
　　My eyes were wet with sorrow's tears.

September 1, 1930

GONE

The yellow moon hangs in the sky
Above the naked silver sea,
While vagrant breezes softly sigh
To stir my longing reverie.

Alone I stand to gaze upon
The scene where once I found content;
In grief I muse, for you are gone,
And with you all the bliss you lent.

Your gentle smile, those saddened eyes
Too beautiful for human brow,
I found in them a paradise—
O God! Could I but see them now!

To read in them a sympathy,
An understanding steeped in love
Which you alone could give to me
As benedictions from Above.

To comfort me and be my guide
When I my hopes and fears confess
Yet roguishly my protests chide
At love's supposed fickleness.

To bear my sorrow as your own
And hide your woes in my distress:
I've lost the helping hand you've shown,
I need you for my happiness.

The full moon pales, the skies turn gray,
Yet still across the sea I stare;
No consolation comes with day—
Alone I wait, and you are—where?

Each night I watch the moon's slow rise
In hope that you'll return to me,
And though with dawn my hoping dies
I have you still in memory.

September 23, 1930

A Fleeting Kiss

A fleeting kiss,
Ecstatic bliss,
Elysian dreams could not enhance;
Then partings, tears,
Dark leadened years,
A lonely soul devoid romance.

September 24, 1930

Her Smiling Face

He was on his way home
From school with his books
Balanced precariously
On the handlebars.

And suddenly they slipped off
Just as he was passing
A group of girls
From his own class.

They all giggled,
As girls do.
All but one
Who ran out swiftly,
Smiled at him,
And replaced the scattered books.

She moved away the next year.

The other girls today
Are caring for
Their children's children,
And the school itself
Is now a parking lot.

But sometimes when
He hesitates before
He steps aside
To let a stranger pass

He sees her smiling face.

In Memoriam — D.S.

There was not in all the country
A finer friend than he
Nor could one ever hope
A better man to be.

His witty cranks amused us all,
His works aroused a deep respect
His moral code a barrier wall
At which all wrong was wrecked.

At his will a clear mind worked
Ne'er at a loss to do or say;
Behind his words a Master lurked
Forming another from model clay.

His silken locks had seen no gray
As he departed for all time
Since he'd but started life's long way
When he faded for the sublime.

What stranger ways are those of God
Whose thoughts we cannot read
Than to bear away from sight to sod
Those whom we are in most need?

Last Night

Last night I felt so lonesome, blue,—
    Don't know just why I was that way,
I guess most people sometimes do
    When all their friends are far away.

It may have been the lonely moon
    Brought memories of silver seas;
Or was it some familiar tune
    Came haunting on a vagrant breeze?

Perchance a catch-phrase clutched my heart,
    Dear words we toyed with constantly.
'Twas true that laugh gave me a start—
    I even turned my head to see.

And then I overheard a name
    Employed by one who did not know
That someone else had used the same
    As tenderly, not long ago.

But now I'm happy, gay again;
    A letter came today—you knew?
But still you hardly blamed me when
    Last night I felt so lonesome, blue.

October 31, 1930

"Goodbye—and Good Luck!"

"Goodbye, and good luck!" was all you said;
A pressure of hands and you had fled.
Carrying with you the laughter and smiles
I needed to lighten the torturesome miles
Of sorrow and strife and breast-laden woe
We each in life's journey too soon learn to know.

"Goodbye, and good luck!"—it rings in my ears,
And I see you there still through a gray mist of tears,
Striving to lighten the burden you guessed
Shrouded my soul in its lost treasure quest,
Breathing unspoken your heart's sympathy
For a fantastic dreamer whose dreams couldn't be.

"Goodbye—and good luck!"—did a sob break the phrase?
Was it by chance you averted your gaze?
Did you know what it was to have dreams break in two?
Was it fancy that made your own eyes seem wet, too?
... Though long we be parted so deep those words struck
I'll always remember: "Goodbye—and good luck!"

November 2, 1930

The Answer

As boys we two would sit and watch by night
The shooting stars blaze pathways through the gloom,
Their coruscations in a flaunting flight
Defying ghosts who haunt their Stygian tomb.

And though we sat as twins in mystery
I envied him his boundless faith and trust,
For he believed in an eternity
For men and stars that was not lost in dust.

But years have passed; alone I watch the sight
Of meteors until their glow is gone.
Effulgent in their blind yet guiding light
I wonder still if they and mortals, dead, live on,

And turn to ask, forgetting he had died,
I feel as certain as if he replied.

April 2, 1931

Sonnet to a Certain Young Lady

O thou resplendent flow'r of changing hue
Diffusing happiness where e'er you stray—
Eternally thy graces burst anew
Yet, unlike blossoms, fail to fade,—but stay
Unchanging in quiescent redolence,
Exquisite in thine every mood divine:
'Til thy perfections even may enhance
Sublime ideal's meticulous design:
And lift thee far above Earth's vulgar sight
To dwell with Virtue's sovereign fixity—
A guiding star, an omnipresent light
Attired in thy benignant probity:
    The while in wonder at thy throne I kneel
    To find in thee transcendency's ideal.

They Did Not Know

He smiled because he loved her so
And did not wish to let her know
That her refusal, taking toll,
Had wrecked a life and crushed a soul.

And she, uncertain in reply,
Half turned to cry what would deny
Her hasty words, but saw his smile
And thought he did care the while.

And thus they parted, she for tears,
And he to carry through the years
A heart devoid of loving glow,
All—all because they did not know.

April 2, 1931

Life's Way

He wished for mansions, servants, gold,
And for them cheated, schemed, and lied,
Until he owned a wealth untold,
Nor ever was his wish denied.

Another had his wishes too:
He dreamed of comfort, home, and wife,
But these as joys he never knew,
Though he fought squarely all his life.

And thus the scoundrel lived in peace;
The "poor but honest" steeped in strife;
In death alone he found release:
How strange are these, the ways of life!

June 12, 1931

The Beggar

A beggar with soul-haunted eyes
Stretched forth a scrawny hand for aid,
And I who deemed myself world-wise, —
I cursed him for the role he played,

And walked on swiftly 'till I met
A woman whose expression wore
An anguish I would not forget:
Her child had died the day before.

And then I linked her fearful stare
As twin in sorrow to that one
Whom I had spurned, and fled to where
I saw him last. But he had gone.

June 12, 1931

Dead Days

Last night came wafted to my ear
A love song of the long ago
A song that made dead days appear
And turned back time's unceasing flow.

Those carefree days, those languid hours,
That crowd of happy-hearted friends
Who little thought, like spring-time flowers,
That summer with its joy soon ends.

We sang our songs, we laughed and played,
And pledged ourselves to pleasure's will;
We faced time's treadmill undismayed
But now both laugh and song are still.

The past is dead, and buried deep
Are all the ties we held as dear
But yet in each those mem'ries creep,
Those haunting thoughts of yesteryear.

But songs and nights soon fade away
As did our friendships' twilight glow,
Yet there remained at break of day
A love song of the long ago.

June 12, 1931
Revised June 17, 1931

Seeking

Away, vain comforter, I know
That careless death has little thought
Of sorrow's countless tears that flow
And that life's lessons were untaught
Had not the heart its taste of woe.

Nor deem it strange some night if I
Should venture forth to seek what men
May dream to find where sea meets sky,
Where past is present once again—
Where lost ones walk and never die.

I would but seek to find relief
From anguish love cannot conceal—
A solace to allay my grief,
So that thru' life I then could feel
A trust in God—divine belief.

I would to glean thru' faith's insight
What reason never can instill,
So that when mortal soul takes flight
I'll recognize God's gracious will,—
And not dark death's eternal night.

June 30, 1931

Confession

You thought I was selfish and fickle, I guess,
And built all my dreams round my own happiness;
You thought that I gloried in laughter and noise,
That I spent too much time with too many boys;
That my love would perish, as love often ends
With me saying, "No, but can't we be friends?"
You thought I was happy when goodbyes were said
That the tear in my eye was a cold in my head;
And tho' there is sorrow in my heart tonight
I'll have to confess, I'm afraid you were right.

October 11, 1931

September 15, 1931

We stopped but for a moment's view,
Yet longed to linger musing there,
But there were others with us who
Found in the scene but nature bare,

Who did not hear in that soft breeze
The murmurings of long-dead leaves,
Nor see upon the lake-lapped shore
The trail to youth's forsaken door.

So we but paused, then went our way,
For we did not expect them to
Find in the silent lake that day
The cherished memories we knew.

October 11, 1931

THE CYNIC'S CHOICE

Some distant day, in some far place
I'll meet my dream girl face to face;
Then, will I hold her cherished charms
In'passioned clasp within my arms
Aflame with love's eternal glow?
You might think so.

                    But I? Hell, no!
I'll turn and flee though I may weep
For I have dreams that I must keep.

October 11, 1931
Revised October 31, 1931

Dark Dawn

You thought I'd sigh when you had gone—
Some men's conceit!
You thought I'd cry into the dawn,
Admit defeat
And come to you with pleading eyes
And honeyed word,
Confess I'm wrong, apologize
For what occurred.

You placed no weight upon my pride
Or righteous wrath;
You thought my love for you denied
A separate path;
You made believe that should I leave
'Twould make you glad.
And while in solitude I grieve—
... I wish I had!

November 7, 1931

Written on a Train

Scores of mortals, seas of faces,
Speeding on white singing rails,
Bound by fate's eternal graces
On the same yet parting trails.

Seated on life's mortal train
In unscheduled trackless flight,
Where trails but meet to part again
And bravely glide into the night.

November 22, 1931

Vale Atque Ave!

He left me even as the night
Slips silently into the dawn;
Left me to wage the losing fight
Of life, with love and lover gone.

Dream castles crushed; — my passion cool —
Well might I wish that I were dead;
But why should I be such a fool
When I have someone else instead?

November 22, 1931

Prom

A pair of dark eyes
Leveled at mine,
A lingering glance—
No other sign,
Just for a moment
Then in between
Us, gliding couples,
Forming a screen—
A barrier wall
To be scaled once more
In an eternal instant
As she paused at the door,
Turned about slowly,
A bird poised for flight,
Gazed softly toward me—
Then was lost in the night—
Left me to dance
And to mem'ry resign
A pair of dark eyes
Leveled at mine.

December 20, 1931

The Meliorist

Many, many years ago
An old man said to me:
"The wisest men are those who know
That every life can be
A song of sweetest melody,
If one will only make it so."

And tho' I've wandered thru' the night
Of woe's dark weariness
And fought the ever-losing fight
In quest of happiness,
Crushed by fortune — nonetheless
It's my belief, that he was right.

December 20, 1931

Fortunate Lady

Fortunate Lady with head held so high
And defiant boast that you've yet to cry
Over love or a lover once held dear; —
You've never yet wrapt your dreams in a tear?

O Lucky Lady with heart as yet free
Has life never played you its melody
Of rapture until, its bow too far bent,
Its discords betrayed a lover's lament?

Never yet writhed in the pang of regret?
Or sought to recall, yet longed to forget?
Never yet gloried in dreams broke in two?
Fortunate Lady — I'm sorry for you.

January 29, 1932
Revised February 9, 1932

The Next to Last Waltz

I sit with my pipe in the moonlight's beam
Wrapt in a veil of smoky blue,
Ecstatically dancing within a dream
Of the next to last waltz with you.

Though I dream alone in the flick'ring light,
And relive my mem'ries anew,
I've you in my arms as you were that night
Of the next to last waltz with you.

No matter what travail, sorrow, or pain,
Or joy that may someday ensue
My thoughts will return to that night again
Of the next to last waltz with you.

Though long we be parted and dried my tears,
Half-hidden the heart-scars we knew,
The haunting music will cling to my ears
Of the next to last waltz with you.

Yet, mayhap someday, we'll return again
And glide to soft music—we two—
Finding bliss in a kiss even as then
In the next to last waltz with you.

July 6, 1932

To a Mouse

All the splendor of the waking dawn
Or serenity when sun is gone,
All the magic of a moonlit night
Or the comfort of home's welcome light,
All the tenderness of baby's arms,
All the rapture of soft music's charms,
All the haunting pains of memory
And the happy hopes of days to be—
Rapture, splendor, magic—all entwine
In the moment when your lips meet mine.

July 20, 1932

Just to Ride—In Memory of June 3, 1932

Just to ride—and ride—and ride
With you seated by my side,
Your hand in mine, our arms entwined
As we down the moonbeams wind;
Headlights gleaming golden bars
Of hope in answer to the stars
Who urge us onward, so it seems,
On—and on—to sweeter dreams.
Shoulder pillowed for your head
(Even when you drive instead);
Two hearts that flame a brighter light
Than two so used to span the night;
And lips that press a challenge bold
To what life's road may yet unfold,
Both confident and satisfied
As thru' the night we softly glide,
You as guide, by my side,
Just to ride—and ride—and ride....

July 30, 1932

Auf Wiedersehen

Goodnight, my love—auf Wiedersehen;
The time to part has come again;
In dry-eyed tears I say goodbye
And leave you so, but you know why—
Tho' really dear, we never part,
We still are one—you have my heart.

Goodnight, my love—auf Wiedersehen—
"Here in your arms I can't remain"
And tho' I leave you as you dance
I take with me our sweet romance
And dream we're dancing still, my dear,
Yet waking, brush away a tear.

Goodnight, my love—auf Wiedersehen—
Once more it's: "Til we meet again."
Too soon those magic moments fled,
Too long our love has been inbred
With parting's heavy laden tears
And vague unrealized futile fears.

Goodnight, my love—auf Wiedersehen—
Some night we'll stroll down lover's lane
And we shall share each sweet caress
In soft unguarded happiness
When fears and griefs no more remain
'Til then, my love—auf Wiedersehen.

August 2, 1932

Goodnight, My Love

Goodnight, my love, the hour is late
And embers die within the grate;
The moon long since has found its bed;
The ashes in my pipe are dead;
But tho' we two are far apart
The flame of love burns in my heart
As faithfully tonight as on
That Night of Nights which saw a dawn
More wondrous far than ever this
Shall be because within your kiss
I found more splendor, radiance rare
Than ever sunrise could compare; —
A dawn with love's soft roseate gleam
That bathed my soul within a dream
Whose waking hours will be sweet
When only once again we meet
And I can hold you close to me —
Your cheek to mine in ecstasy.
And tho' because you're far away
I know no dawn will come with day
In dreams your lips will soon meet mine
And eager arms again entwine
So close your eyes and sleep, and hear
Me whisper low: "Goodnight, my dear."

August 9, 1932

The Night When First We Met

I shall never forget the night we first met
And I bowed a greeting to you,
How little we thought of the tie to be wrought
Before the evening was through.
Our friends who were there were as much unaware
As we of the circling thread
Of Fate working fast that had caught us at last
Which down thru' the moonbeams led
Its gossamer train in a romantic skein
Weaving two hearts into one.
Not even at last when our meeting was past
Did we glean what the moonbeams had done:
How could we have seen what that night would mean
To a future we'll never regret? —
That Love's spark was fanned when you clasped my hand
On the night when first we met?

August 9, 1932

Plea Before Dawn

Grind all our memories into the dust; —
Of crumbled castles on me place the blame —
Sing our songs, share our trails, dear, if you must,
But, please God, call no one else that old pet name.

August 11, 1932

Sonnet to a Former Roommate

I've not forgotten how it was I'd laugh
At you for learning every melody
That Someone sang, —deride the photograph
You talked to when you thought no one would see;
Of how I'd drown your hopes in ridicule,
And lecture wisely when you came in late, —
Upbraid you nightly as "a crazy fool
Neglecting studies for some silly date."
Recalled my jibes when you'd turn ghastly pale,
Expectant, when the phone would ring—
My thoughtless banter when there was no mail—
Too well remembered is most everything.

But as I toss and watch the dawn's light creep
I wonder if some nights you couldn't sleep?

July 9, 1933

Sonnet to E.T.

Do not pity me, my friend, when starting
On your far journey to such lands as I
Shall never see. Rather, at this parting
Wish me success as well — for while you try
To penetrate the Congo's mossy slime
Or scale Merape's molten slopes,
I, fellow seeker in another clime,
Invite a sterner search with higher hopes.
No compass as my guide, nor any star
But one faint ray of fancied light which seems
More hope than guide, so does it fade afar
A phantom in a wilderness of dreams.

Mayhap someday you too will understand
The greater quests than those of some far land.

August 21, 1933

Three Valentines

Query

Silly of me to ask, I guess;
To a failing memory, I confess,
But ask I must, for I forget:
"Was there ever a moon before we met?"

August 12, 1932

To ———

'Twas just a voice
That came to me
From lips that I
Shall never see,
Whose appealing
Roguish tone
Kept me ling'ring
On the phone—
Now half-mocking,
Yet—not quite
Made me wonder
If she might…
But there I go,
I know I'm wrong,
And yet—the way
She sang that song!

But life is full
And trails spread wide,
Tho' some thoughts will
Not be denied
When just a voice
Comes back to me,
A phantom strain
Of melody…

Treasured trinket
Now at rest,
Nestled in
My Memory Chest.

September 17, 1933
2 A.M.

VISE

Beside my hearth I take your letters up
And read again what one already knows
By heart, snatching at dregs within the cup
Where once was nectar that no longer flows.
No tell-tale marks! Consign all to the fire,
(Cremate the body now the soul has fled!)
And wonder then, forgetful 'tis a pyre,
Why flames mount high when the last spark has fled?

Your first so formal note, how quaint it seems!
Them all, —I read each word within the blaze,
A crumbling packet of assorted dreams,
Except the last. Best to avert my gaze.
Too well I know those final lines. Why dwell
Upon my scented passport into hell?

SONNET

Farewell, my love. I voice no final pleas
To make our parting linger thru' the years
As one of stabbing pain and swelling tears —
Kiss me once more beneath the tinseled trees
That saw our love born, blossom, and decay, —
Then say goodbye. Forget the vows we two
Once made beneath the moon: the play is through,
Small use to save a worn-out resumé.
Dismiss the paths we trod, nor use those same
Pet names again — and should we meet by chance
Let's nod and pass — please — with no backward glance:
No need for us to fan a dying flame.

But if, some moonlit night, you find you care,
Seek out these tinseled trees ... You'll find me there.

Revised October 11, 1933

Wisdom

We have clutched at stars dipped in deep desire,
Watched them totter back and fall, lost from sight,
Like crumbling embers of a pulseless fire
That flicker, fade and die within the night.
Together we have sought the moonbeam trails,
A tangled skein of tinseled tapestry
Too soon unraveled when their glamour fails,
A phantom thread of tarnished alchemy.

Let us be wise now — too wise to regret
The urn of dream-dust from a star-sown past,
Cling to each other lest we should forget
The pyres that light the night no dawn outlast,
Rememb'ring heart-strung bows, when bent too far,
Break as the fragments of a falling star.

1933

OUTRACE THE DAWN

From 1941 to 1954

On Reading John Donne

Go to hell to catch the eye
 With which his mistress transfixed him;
Clutch the sun's rays in the sky
 To draw what vapors to the brim
Of cups of wisdom you can quaff, —
And yet you have not Donne by half.

Shake the skeletal hand of death
 And make a brothel of the grave;
From vampires' lungs suck out the breath
 Of alchemy and thus enslave
Impov'rished man with golden tongue, —
And still Donne's secret's not been wrung.

Nail the soul upon the cross
 And writhe till sin is purified;
Purge the precious ores from dross
 And in rebirth know then you've died,
Thus ending where you had begun:
Then you have done, but have you Donne?

March 7, 1941

To Mary on Parting

The hour is late and I shall soon be gone,
So then, my love, come sit and watch with me
The creeping night obliterate the lawn
And saunter up the path, thus setting free
From human eye the pears that line the lane,
And turn the spruce from blue-laced filigree
To purpled sentinels who will remain
To answer when you wish to talk to me.
For I shall really not be gone, you know—
You'll find me in each old familiar book
You glance at when from room to room you go,
Or at the desk beside you in our nook,
Or in the garden weeding with the hoe,
Or at your shoulder when you start to cook.
In love both time and space are now and here,
So in our love I shall be always near.

1943

Some Things There Are

Some things there are that words cannot convey:
The joy, when on a golden summer day
We found a jewel 'twixt the spruces blue,
Fir-set, upon a pear-lined avenue.
But more than that — a home imbued with peace
When calm and love brought sweet release
From worldly strife, and nature's harmony
Bequeathed us dreams of happiness to be.

Outside our home was more that made us stay:
The joy in bird song at the break of day,
The lyric melody of spring-borne breeze,
The love that grows in one for certain trees,
For daffodils and jays, the smell of spring,
For the regret that falling oak leaves bring.
These things we love, for we have found them good;
These things we found about our neighborhood.

But more we found which seemed to make us feel
That only love and friendship's ties are real:
The way our neighbors aid us in distress,
Their thoughtfulness, — they seem to always guess
The proper thing to do when one is most in need,
The sympathetic, self-effacing deed
They each find time to do, yet will not stay
To hear a word of thanks, but rush away.

"A word of thanks," small recompense for those
Whose friendship, op'ning like a summer rose,
Suffused us with their goodness, gave us more, —
A beauty found within another's door.
Oh, we have tried in little humble ways
To show our gratitude, but naught repays
Such philanthropic deeds ... What then to say?
Some things there are that words cannot convey.

February to March 15, 1944

Sonnet to Moloch

These are our young. Take them, O Moloch, nurse
Them in thy way. Their forms construct of steel;
Remove the heart — good soldiers do not feel —
And on their loveless lips implant a curse
On God and man. With poison fill their veins,
So that in gory death their gushing blood
Will soak the earth with venom, like a flood
Of Hell-broth steeped, from which no goodness drains.

And if a few charred forms that once were men
Slip through thy fingers' grasp and live,
It is not that they have more to give
Or that through living life begins again,
But that, like pools of water after rain,
Here war has been, here Moloch left his stain.

Testament to Marilyn

Ah, there! my sweet. No, do not rise. My chair
And all it views are yours, as well you know.
And that your eyes have rested on the bed
Of pansies by the door, the purpled spruce,
The row of daffodils that marks the road —
Sure make the view much sweeter to the eye.
See there is a shred of hemp on yonder oak?
Look close. On it was tested half the strength
Of youth, a gingham semi-circle's arc
That swung from one high joy to higher joy
That only youth refines without alloy.

Your midnight dress becomes you well. It brings
To mind a gown your mother one time wore:
It was a night, so many dreams ago
That only black and white, the cloth and flesh,
Are brought to focus now; there beauty stood:
White pearl upon a velvet cloth of jet,
A radiance surpassing form and face,
Beyond the sense, beyond the mind, and yet
Combining both, surpassing both in some
Unearthly way that made her part of life
And yet above it.

Not a word of this
To her. She knows. Some tapestries the mind
May weave too delicate, ineffable
For tongue to frame, but are transmitted by
An inner sense in words unsyllabled.

Some day, some night, you, too, will understand,
And if that night star-dreams lie in your grasp, —
Stars that still shimmer steadfast in the light
Of day — then clutch them bosom-fast and know
Such dreams, conceived in love, outlast all dawns,
All sorrow-clouded, storm-wreathed skies.

How, now!
Your glance strays out across the green brocade
Of lawn as though if eye were wing my wren
Would now be perched on yon high oaken wood.
Tush now, nor seek to parry soft reproach
With softer arms. Too oft thy mother's arms
Have yoked my neck for me to fall a prey
To fledglings' blandishments! Your glances speak
Warm welcome for a looked-for guest.

But stay
A moment more. He is not come, and if
He were, a little cooling of the heels
Might soothe the burning pace of youth.
Youth speeds adventure's clock as though afraid
The chest of time will empty overnight.
Nor would I say 'tis wrong. To fill the chest
Until the lid is left ajar, until
The chest o'erflows and fills another's cask, —
To load each hour with all the bounty of
The years, a ransom for the Faustian soul,
And yet not barter what was his to sell, —

This is to live. To drink the waters of
The Avon stream of life, to walk the road
To France behind the matchless Florentine,
Upon thy lips the Russian's melody
Of all that heart can give, to be bequeathed
The golden age of Greece, the largesse that
Was Rome's to give, to share the favors of
The nine Parnassian maids of Helicon
And mold with timeless clay a trinket of
The finite hand or mind, —to leave behind
This legacy, —aye, dear, this is to live.

But more there is. To fill the chest, but not
Just for the filling's sake. Instead, to drain
All feeling from each fragile circumstance,
A nourishment of morsels for the mind:
To find a wealth of diamonds in the dew-drenched lawn
At dawn, and paint the sunset's hues upon
The canvas of the mind; each woodland walk
To blaze with new delight, aspiring with
The soaring lark-song of tomorrow's dreams,
Yet not unmindful of arbutus sprigs,
Half-buried, blooming, 'neath last year's dead leaves,—
To feel the pain of moonlight, the caress
Of rain.

And when the cosmic hand plucks that
Most dear and leaves but voidful grief and wells
Of ungushed tears, to bear the leaden cross

Of sorrow as would He, a swelling soul
Transmuting grief to sympathy, and tears
To boundless love, forgetting self, like rain
Upon the sea, the individual loss
A beatific, universal gain.
And when the purpled shadows homeward creep,
And hearth-fires lick a welcome to the hand
Outstretched, to find a careless rhapsody
In idle talk with proven friends of old;
To wander down the trailways of the mind,
Some so familiar, some but half-explored,
Each turn a new delight. And then to burst
Upon some long-forgotten wayside inn
Of thought, half-covered by the jungle maze
Of time, peer through the windows webbed with age
And for a moment walk the hallways of
The past; — to meet old friends, old dreams, old joys,
And sorrows, too, before tip-toeing through
The half-closed door of memory.

And then,
When friends depart and embers crack and die
Upon the grate, to find a seal of love
Upon two lips, a benediction in
The touch of hands, to know that Love and Trust
And Good are to one's soul a universe
Of suns and moons and stars. This is to live.

There is the bell. Go, dance the night away,
And in thy winsome perky way, entwine

His heart with thine. And, yes, one final word:
Outrace the dawn when home you come. Meanwhile
Thy mother's arms will guide me down the lane
Of daffodils, each one a dream come true.
And I shall bless her for her love — and you.

July 1944

Judas

Below me lies Jerusalem, belike
Some long-dead Egypt queen enwrapped in shroud
Of alabaster, half revered and half
Forgot. Siloam, Gihon were her eyes,
Twin pools of ebon mystery;
The Temple was her crown, a brazen sea,
A mirrored moonlit globe, reflecting all
The past and hopeless dreams of us, her kin,
Who beggar-like, with cup bent to the sound
Of ev'ry passing foot, fawn for the alms
The passing Romans condescend to drop.

So here we rot, sun-baked, half-petrified,
Like driftwood on the chartless shores of time.
O palsy-stricken aging Israel,
Is it for this thy blood and tears were shed?
Thy heritage to sift in dust beneath
The godless tread of foreign legionnaires?
Is it for this that on the morrow we
Will slay the Paschal lamb as sacrifice?
Corrupt dissension splits thy tribes which vie
To curry favor with the Roman lord.
Slave have we been before, but never this,
For though the whip may welt the burdened back,
With mind unfettered there was then still hope.
Here mind's enslaved and there's no need for chains:
Jehovah frees but those who would be free.

Were there a Moses or a David here,
The will of God would then be manifest!

Were there a man—, ah, Judas, speak forthright
Unto thyself. A thought unrecognized
But blights the bloom of thine own fruit. Art thou
The master, or the mistress, of thy mind?
Yea, "speak forthright" indeed, for thou dost know
Within thy heart of hearts there is a man,
One who might lift us from this wretched pit
Which we have dug ourselves, could then redress
Our wrongs, redeem our souls, and wrest this land
From Roman sceptre's scourge, if he but would.
The lame are made to walk, the blind to see,
The dead to live again: these has he done,
And doing these, what limits are there to
His pow'r? But still he vacillates as though
Unwilling to unleash his might, if might
Be his, and squanders God-gifts lavishly
Upon a single beggar blind, instead
Of proffering God's vision to the world
Of man.

Meanwhile from Herod's house where dwells
The Roman Pilate comes no sign to force
The issue, though a thousand spears stand by
To punctuate commands. Perhaps, he, too,
Has felt the mystery and fears as yet
To intervene. 'Tis prudence and not love
That has restrained this Caesar's fist, for he
Knows well that with the festal week once past
The fervor of the multitude will fast
Subside, the crowd disperse, and all be lost.

I wonder at the patience of this man
Who draws us to him like the sun the dew.
Would one who works God's will still temporize,
Delay, and let this opportunity,
Like ripened figs unplucked, rot on the tree,
And souls, like seeds, fall dry on barren ground?
Alone, I find no answer; him beside,
I feel no doubts that need be reconciled.
There is a greatness in the man that makes
Each word of his a holy testament,
A benediction in his ev'ry act,
A greatness that belies the man and steeps
The awe-filled mind with thoughts of the divine.

If he be man or more than man: there lies
The sore that festers the Sanhedrin's soul!
This very moment finds them locked in hot
Debate as to what course they'd best pursue.
They hesitate to pass a sentence on
This Nazarene and seize him on the road
Or in the teeming marketplace for what
They call a crime against our God. They know
Full well their legal swords would blunt and trip
Themselves were he to speak a single word
In his defense, that this fiesta crowd,
If played on properly, would make him king,
And turn to ridicule the mouthings of
Sanhedrin, insecure for all its pow'r.
And yet this multitude is so beset
With its own sufferings that it would turn

And curse a benefactor's proffered hand
Were they but shrewdly exorcised.

Meanwhile,
Jerusalem, belike this smooth-browed face
I sit behind, reveals but little trace
Of all the teeming tumult found within,
Where single sparks, a word, a gesture made,
Would fan a holocaust herein. The One
And Seventy know this as craftily
They sit and ponder: how to set the trap?
Or so Anchises says. Their question is not mine
And would I knew it not. Or is it mine?
"A crime against our God," "a blasphemy,"
They charge, and tip the scales of guilt with his
Own words, or so they say. And in a way
Their venomed tongues do not lack verity.
With my own ears I've heard acknowledgment
That God and he are Father-Son, and though
I've seen such miracles as Lazarus
Gives credence to, still back in Nazareth
Are Joseph and his wife. My father's God
Is yet too dear to me to accept all
Without some greater sign. If he be God
Or Son, no matter which, then by his will
This land of ours could soon be cleansed of all
These Roman leper spots which eat our flesh
And waste the vigor of our lives, and they,
Not paltry money-lenders' tables, be
Thus overturned. If he be God, then could

All Israel unite as one, and love,
Not greed, direct our daily enterprise.
If he be God, —but hold! —if he be God
Or truly the Almighty's son, perhaps
This trap the Court of Justice longs to set
Will prove a pit that will ensnare both Great
Sanhedrin and the greedy Roman horde.
For once aroused, what awful power might
He use, if he be God. And if he be
Not God, why then, —why then, —then let him risk
A rank imposter's fate, however much
I love him as a man.

There is a chance,
However slight, that once confronted with
The choice of unleashed wrath, or, say, a meek
Submission to their charges false, he might
Submit to prison bars, forgiving for
Forgiveness' sake. To take the chance! If one
Who knew him were to direct these enemies
To him, then soon would all this turmoil be
Resolved. Perhaps the priests and elders hold
The key to unlock doors that he thus far
Has failed to open, if he has the means.
Could they be used some way, unknowingly,
To force the issues, so that he must act?
But stay! O grievous, monstrous, cunning thought!
Can this be mine, the brain conceiving it?
Were not the motive of such high design,
I'd swear that Satan did beget the seed!

These priests and elders are not innocents,
And well they might both question and distrust
A seeming traitor who so recently
Has been an ardent follower of him
They fear. How best to hide the true intent?
Could I enact a feigned cupidity
That would convince them of a purpose false?
Were I to seek a bounty for the catch—
Say thirty silver coins, or even more—
Then haggle with them so convincingly
When they refuse to pay the larger sum
That all suspicion would then be allayed,
Might they then accept greed as cause enough
For any act, however base it be?
If I know men, they'd not reject the bait.
There is a quiet garden spot he loves
To which he nightly doth repair to pray.
'Tis called Gethsemane. If he be God...

O Great Jehovah, Maker of us all!
The thoughts men harbor are what make them gods
Or less than gods, and ever less! If he
Be God! There are no doubts in Matthew's mind
Or John's to make them sicken in their souls
Or feel the weight of lead that loads my breast,
The knifing questions that dissect my mind.
These followers who with me form the Twelve
Have neither mind nor soul enough to sense
A God if God there were to walk the road
From Jericho. They are a squirming lot

Of simple Galilean fish soon caught
In any net that meshing minds devise.
Yet such is my own mind belabored
That pity suckles envy till I wish
Their childlike faith were mother to my thoughts.
There is a healing balm in wide-eyed faith
That all the fumbling philosophic twists
Of logic fail to satisfy. And this
I lack, and lacking thus, am blinded to
The light that guides their blinking, mindless eyes.
If Reason were the eye to Truth, then would
I pierce the mists of theologic doubt,
Shear falsehood from the sacrificial lamb,
And cleanse the altar of fallacious blood.
If Right were day and Wrong were night then would
There be a sun to clear this gloom that half
Reveals and half conceals the truth. Instead,
The twilight of the mind lies thick about
This teeming brain, which yet sits spurless on
My body's lethargy. What course? Which choice?
Well is it said that mind malingers mind,
Feigns illness to itself, disports the fool,
And turns the veins' hot liquid flow of deeds
Into a turgid, paralyzing ooze
Of vapid thought. Far better be it that
Man sail his bark straight-forth, directed if
Directionless, to spit on rocks of chance,
Than have it wallow listlessly upon
A windless sea of still-bound dread and doubt.

Yet here I sit and muse the previous hours
Away, unmindful, seemingly, that scales
Of right and wrong may lose their counterpoise
Tonight, and bury dying Israel
Forever in her dust. Oh, Judas, wert
Thou suckled on a jackal's milk, bequeathed
As legacy a herd of sheep-like thoughts
As tim'rous as the foes you vilify?
What gain is there if Judas lives and what
He lives for dies? Within thy hand is held
The choice: to force the issue, prodding destiny,
With hope that Israel will thus be saved,
Or hold the hand and let thy people sleep.

This flaming choice consumes my ev'ry thought
And act. My brain is seared, my body burns,
My soul slow turns to ash ... but in the ash
There lingers yet one spark ...

Gethsemane.

1943 to 1944

Mood

There is a stilly dark tonight
    Where only silence will intrude
For World, like stars, has taken flight
    Behind low clouds of solitude.

And so the backward page again
    I turn to thoughts the years refined,
While memories, like spring-borne rain,
    Run down the roof-eaves of my mind.

1945

Vision Revisited

Some day I hope that we can walk
The roads which I once walked alone
And with insatiable talk
For separation's loss atone.

Then will I lead you by a stream,
Point out a woodland path or two,
Revisiting a treasured dream
That once was vision, now is you.

July 1946

SOUVENIR

Across the dark cuartel of reverie
The sound of taps echoes a memory,
And as the after-glow of time long gone
Dies in the embers of another dawn,
By its dim light come read a page or two
And reminisce on those we one-time knew.
And as you read, no doubt once more you'll see
A face forgot, and hear, "Remember me?"

Remember Rodgers—but then, who'd forget?
I wonder if he took his furlough yet?
And Smith who, when we're all no more alive
But in St. Peter's Room Two Twenty-five,
Will turn about and with a benign smile
Tell one of us to get some major's file!
And Charlie Baker who was Able too;
BLOCK LETTERS were the things that made him blue.
And Fine and Maletz at their Harvard best
Composing questions for the AA Test.
And Quinn, who, playing fireman, caused great ire:
Mixed up our bedding, never found the fire.
And Blau who kept the hopes of some alive
Prescribing Six-fifteen dash Three-six-five.
And Witt who wagered soap on ev'ry bet—
No doubt he's wishing that he had some yet!
And Helen Granstrom's gay infectious laugh
That always seemed to cut our cares in half.

And when the daffodils are first in bloom—
The way that Connie walked across the room.

Remember Rusch so oft Atlanta bound,
But what he did we never heard a sound—
Mel Allen, Keplinger, and Radcliffe Hall,
Who got the air for any cause at all—
Greg Olney, Lady, Adams, Dobberstein:
What memories those names combine!
Bill Evans haunting phone booths whene'er blue:
A call collect to his own Mary Lou.
While Noah Blosser, hunter of great fame,
Hit ping-pong balls instead of game.
Don Simmelinck, once hidden down the hall,
Became a doctor at the slightest call
And almost lost his stripe when asked (right quick)
By You Know Who, "Say, what is this, a trick?"
While Watson daily made us mop his side
And then gave fatherly advice at Eventide.

Remember Sully, Wagers, Kamiak,
And some whose names I even lack—
Don Brady, who although he was no simp,
Forgot on which leg he should always limp—
Tex Johnson, who had never seen a steer,
Could throw the bull but not hold down a beer—
"Casbah" Awadi, whom all grammar foils,
Who got fried eggs instead of "densing goils."
And then there was the great Lord Fauntleroy,
Th' Ambassador from Brooklyn's son and joy.
Remember Miriam and Eleanor
And Sue Outz who were valiant to the core,

Whose cheer and courage without sign of tears
Helped each of us throughout the creeping years.

Remember, oh remember, all those things
To which in retrospect some laughter brings: —
The Journal dance for which the Ocs paid
The night that Loman sang his serenade —
And Mrs. Holloway, who made each one
At ease, then deftly guided all the fun ...
The deathless slogan that no time will blur:
"We need more counsel and less Oliver!"
The time that Bromberg thought he wanted pie
But had to substitute what passed for rye —
The pungent jokes and quips, the famous yarns
Of that team Palmer, Morlock and old Barnes —
The projects Uncle George would have us write:
To think them up he must have spent the night!
The blackjack games out at B-17
When Applebaum who neatly sloughed the queen —
The time that Cronin thought the war was won
Until Old Overholt slowed up his fun —
And there were those to whom (if in the wise)
The Dawning Vision was no mere sunrise!
The Chapel on a moonlit Georgia night
Where Stan Bird's music brought us all delight.
At last each one has gone his sep'rate way
And put behind the cares of yesterday,
And left no mark within the bare cuartel
Except the thought of friends who wish him well.

But if you listen you will hear them call:
"A very Merry Christmas to you all!"
And then their voices reach you once again
To pray: "Peace on the Earth, Good Will to Men!"

Christmas 1946

High Tide

Your arm in mine, we walk the beach again
And watch the moon-drenched spume sweep up the shore,
Erasing with each wave our footprints, then
Retreating, then advancing evermore.

So let us both be wise and wrest the dream
From out the unplumbed strivings of our might,
Full knowing that our evanescent scheme
May not outlast the magic of the night, —

That far away on yet another shore,
Blind to the knowledge that the hour is late,
Man madly builds the barks of total war
To launch them on a final sea of hate

Unmindful that his is a mortal hand,
That tides of time leave no marks in the sand.

August 7, 1947

Through the Years—To My Mother

So many times I've meant to say
The thoughts that burgeon from my heart
As though by words I might repay
The debt I owe, at least in part,

To you who, steadfast through the years,
Despite the costs which you defied,
Through laughter, sorrow, hopes and fears
Have been to me both staff and guide.

You always seemed to sense aright
The substance of my childhood dread:
Outside my door is still the light
To quench the dark where fears are fed.

No task too great, no trivial plea
Failed to enlist your sympathies,
As when you walked to school with me
And when at meals we'd count the peas!

And when my needs the years refined
And guidance turned into advice,
Your wisdom and your love combined
To give me values beyond price.

You took within your hands the clay
And moulded it of such design
So that what faults I have today
Are not your making but are mine.

And when I'd drop a thoughtless word
That hasty tongue could not recall,
It was as though you hadn't heard;
All understood, forgiven all.

Down through the years, when near or far,
You've been the courage that I seek,
My compass when there was no star,
My source of strength when I was weak.

There are no deeds, there is no way
My swelling gratitude to show,
I can but hope that I'll repay
My children for the debt I owe.

So in their growth that you will see
The influence that you have had
In making them as I would be
A tribute to both you and Dad.

Christmas 1947

On Your Birthday

What could I wish you on this day
Of days if I had but the pow'r?
To rub Aladdin's lamp, let's say,
Or wish upon a falling star?

Then would I wish you love each day
And fortune, health and happiness,
But you would smile and in your way
Confide to me these you possess.

And so my wish to you must be
A simple one time cannot mar:
To you, my dear, I make this plea:
To always stay just as you are.

Kynos

I found in you the sympathy
I needed when the world turned black;
Within your eyes turned up to me,
I read devotion others lack.

So brave and loyal, staunch and true,
Unchanged by mood, — a catalogue
Of virtues found alone in you.
I sure am glad I own a dog.

Plexus

Weave the web of all your doing
        Or undoing, and once done,
With dimming eye and trembling finger
        Trace each thread across the loom
Of years and mark your destination, —
        How the lines have crossed and recrossed
To plait your life-span's pattern.

And at such crossing pause and ponder:
        Had the thread, now fixed forever,
Changed its course upon the cloth,
        Spun off in a new direction,
Spun a new and novel pattern,
        What then of your life's design?
Would the basic form have altered?
        Would the thread have changed its color?
Would the cloth be priced much higher?

Or would the form be still this form,
        Thread this thread and cloth this cloth?
Would the interwoven lines when finished,
        Despite the changes wrought in fervor,
Greed or hate or love or hope,
        Indecision or decision, —
Would these lines that mark your fate
        Run parallel yet twine at last
And be this pattern's pattern?

Shots At Random

Prospect

If this is where we are today,
I'm glad I went the other way.

Confession

Let's find out where the facts belong
Before we get into a fight;
I'd like to be as sure you're wrong
As I am sure I'm right.

Birds of a Feather

A hawk and a dove sat in a tree
And argued and fought so fearfully
You could only tell if you knew before
Which wanted peace and which wanted war.

An Gnawful Thought

What happens to the cannibals
When they to hell are sent?
Are they crammed full of vegetables
To make them all repent?

Or must they munch an empty bone
In order to atone,
Or even worse might be their curse,
To gnaw upon their own!

BROCARD

A geophagist
Will never be missed,
But, if you've euphoria,
Let's see some moreaya.

You Are My Valentine

Though you stand there at the sink
Dressed in gingham not in mink,
Though you sweep into a room
Not in brocade but with broom,
Though no gold bedecks your arms
It would only hide their charms,
Though your Cadillac's a Ford
Still remember you're adored
And I wish you'd give a sign
That you'll be my Valentine.

You have built on fruitful loam
Not a mansion but a home
And the three-fold prize within
Glen and Carol, Marilyn,
Fashioned them with loving care
So that wealth cannot compare—
So that gold and brocade fade
When comparison is made.
So as my heart and yours entwine
I know you are my Valentine.

The Calling of General Moore

Some times there are that try men's souls,
When sane men lose their reason,
And one such time in Washington
Is called the Budget Season.

When brave men march up to the Hill,
Each one a valiant person,
And then march back, a wiser man,
A ravin' and a cursin'.

But there is one who never quails,
Steel-hearted to the core, —
Yes, there is one who never fails:
His name is General Moore.

And so it is each passing year
When hearings have begun,
Each witness squirms and wonders
If he should fight or run.

When the House is in a dither
And the Senate's in a sweat,
Each witness seems to wither
And to mumble and forget.

And the Secretaries mutter,
And their hair turns into gray,
And the Generals blink and stutter
And just seem to fade away.

When they mix appropriations
With expenditures,
They'd rather eat K rations
On long Korean tours.

And Admirals and Captains, too,
Wish they were Naples bound,
While Air Force men with all their wings
Can't seem to leave the ground.

Then voices rise much higher
As the Chairman's gavel's swung,
And may barely miss the witness—
A hero, but unsung.

And a Member shakes a finger
At each witness in his turn,
And cries, "We'll get the blasted answers
If we never do adjourn!"

And questions from the Members,
They pile up by the score;
They do not pause for answers,
They just keep asking more.

Then telephones start ringing
As they've never rung before
And the word goes out they're bringing
The man who knows the score.

Oh, bring him in a hurry,
Yes, bring him in before
They stop fringe benefits entirely,
Yes, bring in General Moore!

Then the witness sits much straighter
And the Senators relax,
For they'll hand that hot potato
To the man who's got the facts.

So he strides into the hearing
With assurance in his gait,
And his words are followed closely,
For his statements carry weight.

He'll agree with every question
With a nod that answers, "Yes."
But when they read the record,
It's anybody's guess.

He handles facts like pilots
Performing inside loops;
He marshals words like generals
Commanding well-trained troops.

And he parries every question
With an answer so devised
That no blame can fall on any
And yet it's so disguised

That one side thinks that it has won
A point that, undenied,
The other side had held throughout, —
And both are satisfied!

And so the hearing's over,
But no Member leaves before
He shakes the hand of that sage man,
Major General Moore.

So when the final roll is called
At some far distant date,
And each of us now living
Has gone to meet his fate,

Then maybe you and I will knock
Upon the Pearly Gates
And St. Peter bids us pause and then
Each one interrogates.

Perhaps we'll try to answer
And perhaps we won't do well
And we'll have a fleeting vision
Of where we soon might dwell.

'Tis then, we hope, the same old cry
Will echo down through time
And angels in a chorus
Will chant the same old rhyme:

"Oh, bring him in a hurry
Before the Pearly Door
And let him take the witness stand—
Yes, bring in General Moore!"

And he will come in breathless,
(But what's that to a shade?)
The answers that he gives will help
Some spirit make the grade!

In years to come there may be those
Who'll win as great applause,
And then again there may be those
Who'll fight as great a cause.

But there will never be a man
More kindly in his heart
Whose understanding sympathy
Is without counterpart.

And never will there be a man
More honest brave and true;
The Purple Heart they gave to him
Provides but just a clue.

No, there will never be a man
More forthright to the core,
No finer soldier ever walked
Than our own Bobby Moore.

1954

OUTRACE THE DAWN

From 1960 to 1968

Cafeteria Blues

The table ain't the same, man,
Since you went away.
There ain't a single dame, man,
Who makes us look her way.

Farrell squirms upon his chair
And John forgets to blow his smoke,
Maurie swears he'll cut his hair
While Harold's stock has gone for broke.

Ken no longer sits till noon,
The sights for Mike no more are fun,
While Al finds records out of tune
And even Fran forgets to pun.

We miss the leader of our group,
Your subtle observations.
We miss your double plates of soup,
Your gripes about the rations.

When worldly issues are on trial,
We miss your ratiocination;
When pretty girls walk down the aisle,
We miss your quick gyration.

For Maurie, Harold, Farrell, Fran,
John and Al and Mike and Ken
Won't be happy till we can
Hear your "huba" once again!

Washington

The invitation
To the embassy reception
Lay buried in the correspondence
That accumulates
From day to day.
Forgetting it
Was unintentional,
For I had thought to go.

There was a time that I would pass
That high-walled edifice
And envy those who
From black limousines
Emerged to disappear inside,

Just as, long ago,
Applying my lipstick
For the first time
I longed to visit,
The mansion that stood
On the top of the hill
Back home.

But today,
Inured to views
From higher peaks,
I jot them on my calendar
And try to work them in.

Yet as I do so,
Pause and ponder,
And note that somewhere on the way
I've lost the wide-eyed dawn
Of yesterday.

1960

Written for a Precious Moment

As we look down the tides of time
And mark the ledger sheet of years,
We find the blessings far outweigh
The grief, the pain, the loss, the tears.

And as we count the joys of life,
We find in them a treasure chest
To share, yet in the sharing keep
Forever in the owner's breast: —

A passage in a book once read,
A log-fire's thought-provoking glow,
A sympathy in words unsaid,
The symmetry of flakes of snow,

The love of those we hold so dear,
The pounding surf, its ebb and flow,
A helping hand in time of stress
A phrase of music, long ago,

The fragrance of a single rose,
The laughter of a little tot,
A woodland path that is no more,
A gift the giver's long forgot.

And I will treasure all of these
And more. For in that laden chest
I place this precious moment with
Those cherished friends I love the best.

February 20, 1960

Sonnet on the Construction of Interstate 95

Here yesterday the lovely dogwood grew,
Protected by majestic oak and pine,
Here cardinal and thrush and pheasant, too,
Sought forage by the scarlet columbine.

Here long ago the Powhatan's quick feet
Sped silently along a woodland trail
With tautened bow his ready aim to meet
The elk, the deer, the partridge and the quail.

But now the forest is a vast array
Of edifices rising to the stars
And trails are highways structured to display
A constant stream of plangent motor cars.

While just above a solitary tree
A lonely bird sings nature's threnody.

The Plum

A plum.

You have seen it there
For ever so long
Admired it
Cherished it
Coveted it.

Now reach for it
Stretch out for it
Until you think your guts will burst
Ignoring failure
Persisting
Knowing beyond knowing
You'll get it
In the end.

And when you do
Spend no more
Than a moment
Savoring its flavor
But use it
To help those
You love
And those
You do not know
To reach for
Their plum.

And find
In so doing
This is your real plum
Rich beyond price.

Portrait

This is his final portrait over here.
As you come up the stairs you cannot miss
The feel of it. His enemies insist
He picked the spot himself. I like to watch
The tourists as they clamber up the steps,
Most chattering like monkeys in a zoo,
And when they see him as you do—but there—
You follow what I was about to say.
It's known to be the artist's masterpiece,
Or so I've heard the other guides repeat.
I have no critic's eye to praise or blame
The artistry, and I have looked so long
At this same canvas that my memory
Of him and it are intertwined so that
This is his face as far as I recall,
Although I'll say this was not always so.

They put the painting just beside those two
About whose greatness there can be no doubt,
Or if dispute there ever was, long since
The distillation of the years has left
No residue. There still are those alive
Who bristle at his name as though 'twere salt
Upon a wound, although if they were but
To look, they'd fail to find a single scar,—
Or so it's said. I am not paid to judge
And those who judge are judged, or so I've heard.
To those who know us best we never are
As tall as men of whom appraisal is
The residue of reputation's glow.

The mountain towers highest from the plain
And saints are only saints once they have died.

It never did occur to most of us
To think of him as of a stature to
Bring down the homage of the multitude—
At least, I think this true until he died.
We tend to minimize men's attributes
Until the breathing stops. Then suddenly
The legends start to multiply and cults
Of new believers magnify the good
Until all semblance of him as he was
Is lost forever, or perhaps until
Another cult of idol-breakers pull
The statues down—and there's still time for that.
Stand over here. Maybe it is the light,
The way it gives a certain lustre to
The eye and down the cheek, or yet again,
Perhaps the artist's brush has caught some thing
That only those who seek it out may find.
Communication may well be the key
To both the portrait and the subject's fame.
So many of us try to send out waves
That never are received, or if received,
Are garbled in the sending so that we
Can never be quite fully understood
And all we strive to say and do is lost.
There was a time that I aspired—but there—
They tell me we are paid to recite facts,
Though what are facts was never clear to me.

I do not know what makes for greatness in
A man, or what, at least, the scales of time
Pronounce as such. So much there is that must
Depend on winds of chance, or circumstance
That's not design. And yet some prescience in
This man enabled him to spread or reef
His sails accordingly and catch the gale
That threatened to engulf his ship so that
He'd bring it safely to his chosen port.

He had a courage that few men possess,
Nor speak I now of common bravery
Where a decision must be made upon
An instant's notice. No, such is not hard
To find, where one risks life or cause almost
Without a thought despite the fancied odds.
But rather he was one who weighs the odds
And ponders the alternatives, discerns
Broad avenues of compromise wherein
An almost-goal may be achieved without
The risk, and seeing all this then elects
To plunge ahead audaciously while men
With softer spines cringe supinely and fill
Their lungs with fear. We praise such strong resolve
And rightly, too, I guess, but is this sword
Not double-edged, in that the argument
Is rarely tipped so far that right and wrong
Are not enmeshed in either side so that
A compromise serves all in better stead?

You'll note the guard who stands by yonder arch.
'Tis prudence and not happenstance that puts
Him there. If you look close, you may discern
The center of the canvas has been patched
Where once an object thrown in hate and haste
Just missed the face. A pretty penny was
The restoration cost. No matter now.
In time this blemish may well disappear.
Some say he, too, was flawed — and who is not? —
In that he loved not men but all mankind,
And in pursuing this yet larger goal
He trod upon ambitions even though
The wearers never hoped to match his stride.
We rarely guess the fears that haunt the minds
Of harried men, not how the drum-tight mask
Of skin conceals the throbbing tumult checked
By muscles, taut in graven discipline.
I wonder did he ever walk the floor
Of anguished doubt and question motives, goals,
And even self, if conscience still prevailed?
Or can it be ambitions cancel doubt,
That there's no room for both in mortal frame?
Perhaps the fawning adulation of
The multitude veneers the skin and coats
The finer senses with a glaze that robs
Them of the common touch, so that the warmth
Of nature dissipates, and all that's left
Is the hard shell where once compassion flowed.
There is no prison cell to match the mind
That conjures fancied bars to chain the brain.

He had a unique presence of command.
The tourists seem to sense this aura of
Authority, though oil and pigment are
Poor substitutes for flesh and bone.
I've seen them come direct from out of doors,
Gaze intently, then shift their eyes away
But to return as though compelled to meet
The master's stare. I've even watched them bare
Their heads almost unknowingly, then look
About shame-faced, to see if they're observed—
Awed part by art and part by legend's lore.
In later years when he walked in a room
There'd be a pause, a comma in the speech
Of those who faced the door, as though there were
For just a nonce a mental shift of gears
That checked the words in some mute tribute's rite—
Cerebral genuflection to the man—
Or slowed them down, as one decelerates
When signals warn with caution to proceed,
Or there's no guide to mark the road ahead.
It could have been the weight subjection spawns
In those most apt to feel the heavy load.

He was a leader even as a boy—
Or so I've read somewhere—and early quaffed
The heady brew of dominance that brooked
No challenge or a shade of compromise,
A greed for power that seemed to consume
His ev'ry act and left unquenched his thirst,
Although so mixed was it with higher aims,

'Tis hard to say for certain if it were
Some altruistic means that were the end
And not the other way about. Who knows?
I do not know what chemistry combines
Within a man's make that triggers such desire—
Perhaps a striving for the striving's sake,
Or are there arcane seeds that grow within
The human breast and gnaw for dominance,
Fed by ambition, rivalry and fame?
What matter now? Somebody has to lead.
Now he is gone, as are the hopes of those
Who dared to doubt omniscience in this man.

I've often wondered if he had a friend.
You look surprised. The friends he made before
He reached the top soon found a message in
The frozen smile and hackneyed phrase he deigned
To proffer when perchance their paths recrossed.
Or do I wrong the man? Beset he was
Each moment by pressing multitude
Of problems to be solved, decisions to
Be weighed and made, and rival forces to
Be balanced or unbalanced with a nod
Or studied stratagem, he scarce had time
To pause to voice amenities as such,
Not even for the sake of times gone by.
But then he lacked not those who sought to call
Him friend, for such use as the word is worth.
When fame once knocks, up pops a mighty host
Of hangers-on, like mushrooms overnight,

Whose deferential bow and enforced laugh
Betrayed them for the sycophants they were.
The only friends of whom we can be sure
Are those we had before we won the prize.
When there is much to gain, how can one pan
The gold from all the dross of humankind?

We're paid to say the picture's frame came from
A tree he climbed in when a boy, a tree
That lightning felled the day he died.
I've seen that tree—I know it well—and it
Still stands, as though to make a mockery
Of all the golden tributes we recite.
One wonders how much credence can be placed
In much of what they mouth as history.
In truth there is no history as such,
But just the thesis of the winning side.

There is the closing bell. The stairs are to
Your right. So many times he used those steps
Himself, belike an ordinary man,
When one must leave, there are no separate
Exits for the great.
                                        Thank you, sir, you're kind.

The Silver Years

The silver years which we together spent
Have not been spent but will forever be
A priceless hoard, refined, preeminent,
Within my treasure chest of memory.
And I shall count them over miserly
And hold each one more precious than the last
And cherish all the shining moments we
Have stored within the mind-vaults of the past.
And in the counting gratefully I'll find
A wealth of tokens of your tender care
And understanding which we two combined
To form the love and happiness we share,
And share yet more than wealth could ever be:
The three-fold heritage you gave to me.

September 3, 1963

Lines on a Lost President

Like to a towering oak etched high
Against the framework of the sky,
One moment there, then there no more,
Hewed to the earth almost before
The growth was done, leaving a void
Of anguished sorrow, unalloyed,
A loss too great to be defined
Within the hearts of all mankind.

Then let this loss be not in vain,
That sacrifice be turned to gain,
And those high goals for which he fought
Be not allowed to come to naught:
As with his banner still unfurled
We strive to build a better world.

Looking Backward

We slowed our speed and sent our craft
Skimming above the surface of the land.
All about us the earth lay bare
And naked with no vestiges of life.
There was no tree nor living creatures,
Neither those which walk,
Nor those which crawl,
Nor those which fly.
As far as eye could see
The land was gray and bleak,
The only movement being that of clouds
Which drifted down the sky
Quite aimlessly, as though without a home.
Here and there was ample evidence
That once a society
Had flourished, bloomed and then withered.
Tall edifices poked their crumbled spires
Above the drifting sands,
Huge holes pock-marked the terrain,
About which metal fused with stone
Were married in a rubble heap.
So with the coming of the dusk
We set our sights on that far distant twinkling light
From whence we came, and as we did so wondered
What sudden holocaust
Had brought this planet to its death.

May 18, 1964

The Vase

It was a small glass vase
Of no real value,
The kind you hang
Upon a wall
And deck with rosebuds
When they are in season.

He had purchased it
Because it caught his eye
And for no other reason.
And through the years
It hung upon the wall
And had been peopled
With countless guests
Who had their hour
And then departed.

He never spoke of it to her,
Perhaps because it was
Not worth the mention,
Perhaps because he felt
His attachment to it
Unexplainable or effeminate.

And when he died
It hung there still
Until she moved to smaller quarters,
When it was stored away.
And when the children
In their time

Divided what was left,
Made disposition of the goods
For which they had no use,
It disappeared, as such things do,
For who would keep
A small glass vase
Of no real value?

July 1964

Boarding House Blues

How much am I bid
For a second hand id
When the juice of the turnip is fled?
Does the matrix of time
Have a meter or rhyme,
And will somebody please pass the bread?

We administer doses
Of Type O psychosis
Till ratiocination is dead,
While we anodize men
With a jigger of Zen—
Can't we ever have meatballs instead?

Cybernetic studies
Make you and me buddies,
With punch cards we seek whom we'll wed.
In existential ease
We'll do as we please:
Must we eat the lower-priced spread?

With a payload of fission
We start on our mission
To make the world dread what we dread,
While with syndromes of hate
Men shoot craps with fate.
These potatoes are heavy as lead.

At a Mach Three pace
We annihilate space,
Got a cure for a cold in the head?
Let's capsulate college
With instant knowledge.
Your sleeve's in my salad, he said.

We'll all become free
With a world empathy
Of red, white and blue or just red,
So just exercise right
And exorcise might,
But who's going to dole out the bread?

April 28, 1965

THE KITCHEN

No need to call on Woman's Lib
Or argue about Adam's rib;
No cause for any court opinion:
This room is woman's sole dominion.

In this her room's periphery
She conjures modern alchemy,
Transmuting with a pot or mold
Viands to delicious gold.

A room of creativity
Depending on proclivity,
A treasure trove, a sometimes bar,
A clubhouse or a cookie jar,

Perhaps a daily cross to bear,
A picnic ground for one to share,
Disposal and trash can combined,
The garbage pail of humankind,

A magnet with such awesome pow'r
It draws small fry every hour,
The proper place for mud to track,
The place to steal a midnight snack,

A meeting ground for young and old
To forage food that's hot or cold,
Where gourmets, gluttons both agree
On food for thought's democracy,

And yet a room of solitude
Where even dreams sometimes intrude …
So if you'd track me to my lair,
Look in this room. You'll find me there.

1967

On Reading Dorothy Eddy's Poems

Dainty trinkets of the mind,
Braille book for the social blind;

Bird song soft at eventide,
Doors of vision open wide;

A vintage quaff from yesteryear,
Prismatic structure of a tear;

Diagnoses, sutures, knife,
Ministering to the ills of life;

Puckish whimsy, worldly care,
Touch of dream-stuff, soul laid bare;

Portrait gallery of our time
In a golden frame of rhyme.

January 17, 1968

Recognition

At first I did not recognize him.
He strode along brusquely,
Elbowing his way through the crowd,
Stepping quickly through the door
Before those who had been waiting.
Only when he turned did I recognize
Him as one whose name was famed
In his field for the beauty
And delicacy of his art.

March 8, 1968

On Reading Emily Dickinson

Pristine fragile flower
        Born to blush unseen,
Locked within her chamber
        With the Golden Mean.

Never had a loved one,
        Few could call her friend,
Though her love encompassed
        World without an end.

Rarely rubbing elbows
        In confraternity,
Yet steeped in worldly wisdom's
        Dark profundity.

Bound by social strictures,
        A bird that cannot fly,
Yet verse on verse goes soaring
        In a cloudless sky.

Ragged lines lack polish
        With meter breaks and failing rhyme
That introduce a vision
        Of ageless truths, defying time.

Nature's keen observant handmaid,
        Friend to butterfly and bee,
Giving falling leaves and snowflakes
        Immortality.

Innocent of metaphysics,
Novice in religious lore,
But certain of a Godly welcome
When she knocks on Heaven's door.

Haiku Poems

I

Nature's perfection:
Symmetry of a snowflake.
Where is man's design?

II

The wind grows bold
And the oak bends with the gale,
Then stands straight again.

III

A lone nest-bound bird
Flees across the darkling sky
To outrun the night.

IV

Quietly a leaf
Falls to earth to be dust-ground
To nurture its kin.

V

Omniscient gulls dive
Upon the tell-tale ripple
In the placid sea.

VI

Brooks flow into streams
And thence into the oceans.
May not souls to God?

VII

Translucent sun rays:
A white veil from earth to sky
Bedeck nature's brides.

VIII

The mountain fingers
Stretch to pierce the secrets of
The retreating blue.

May 11, 1968

From 1971 to 1979

A Commodious Ode

All blessings on thee, room of rooms
Most intimate, yet most austere,
Where all assume an equal pose
And everyone is judged a peer.

The crowning boon to all mankind,
The answer to the stranger's plea,
Symbol of the civilized state,
Reminder of mortality.

A room the source of limpid pools,
Where showers in a spring-like mist
Descend to cleanse the dermal sheath, —
All done with magic flick of wrist.

A room that's privy to our hopes,
Escape valve for our worst distress,
A seat of striving, throne for all,
That's flushed with each success.

Sole confidante of truth laid bare,
From whom no secret we may bar …
So paeans to thee, canny friend,
Who knows us as we really are.

1971

A Room With a View

"A room with a view, please,"
Was all I said, hoping my voice
Was strong and full. I signed
The flourished register
As though it were a commonplace.
He took the pen and eyed my name
As though to drain it of all ancestry.
"Will you be staying long?"
"Well, for a time, at least.
My plans are not yet firm."
My smile came back in smaller change.

> For a time at least. A night, a year
> Or an eternity. How firm are any plans?

He said, "We have a fine suite
On the topmost floor from which to see it all—
The city and the mountains, too."

> There is no suite on earth
> From which to see it all. And yet
> We keep on searching, hoping still
> To find the panoramic key.

"And the price?" And as I spoke,
I knew as well as he that they
Who ask cannot afford the view.

Must price and view be intermeshed
Through all the questing years?
And how to measure price?
The drudging labors of a lifetime spent?
Or just a coupon cut with regularity?
Or having relatives or friends
To pass the word at the right time?
Or higher still, dissimulation
And chicanery when price is right
Or when hard pressed to hold one's own?

Hesitation is its own reply.
"Or do you wish a single room?"
His voice was much too casual
To reflect the import of the query's thrust.
"Why, yes. Of course. I'm traveling alone."
My answer's placid tone surprised
Some quivering trigger in my mind.

Of course I'm traveling alone!
Had I have had a retinue of followers
The answer would have been the same.
Must not we all go forth alone,
Regardless of the ones we love
And who love us, however much they long
To hold our hand forevermore?
And is this not the sorrow of creation's plot,
That each, so soon or late, must bear
To share with none the solitude
Of the last crannies of the mind?

He said, "We have a room
That's on the northern side.
Not quite as large, but adequate.
A splendid view." He found a key
That looked like all the rest.

> Must price prescribe the view?
> And who decides its splendor?
> And must it be a lifetime spent
> Within a sunless room?
> And this decision, is it mine,
> And what will it decide?
> And still again, what cost?

He rang a bell and tossed the boy
The key. His voice no longer
Gave off warmth. The elevator's lift
Pulled at my legs. We reached the door,
A twin to every other door
Along the long dark hall,
A room, just like the rest no doubt,
And yet unique, for it was to be
Mine alone.

> Why must all doors appear alike?
> And who's to tell what's on the other side?
> Or does it really matter?
> For are all rooms what occupancy makes,
> Or are they, in the end, identical?
> And who's to say I do not share

My room with transient guests
Long since departed from the scene,
As well as that long list
Of others yet to come
Who'll share with me
The essence and the secrets of this room?

The key clicked in the lock
As though to register another occupant.
The door creaked open inward,
And I, amalgam of the hopes and fears
Accruing in the mold of time,
Edged in the opaque space beyond.
Wondering as I did so
If the key fits any other door.

Bicentennial Hymn

O, say can't you see that we want to be free
From all that we sought in the past?
What so proudly we hailed, we may now have failed,
But at least we will have quite a blast.

In our schools we can't pray, but that's just a way
To make sure that we will be free.
Religion's outmoded and home life eroded:
Three cheers for our new liberty!

With our morals unglued, we parade in the nude
For porno's our motto today.
Let's be sure to be glib about all kinds of Lib
And be swingers and swappers and gay.

Through the law's alchemy we'll set murderers free:
Want to walk in the street after dark?
If we can just wheedle a trip with a needle
Then the future will be just a lark.

We should greet with elation unbridled inflation
While the dollar shrinks almost in half.
We'll send wheat to Russia, so they can live plusha
We always can live on the chaff.

Since there's no quick solution to combat pollution,
Let's ignore the air, land and sea.
We can squander resources, —we might find new forces
To harness the earth's energy.

With a Concorde or two, we'll fracture the blue
And be nowhere in half of the time,
And we'll fill up the air with the missiles' red glare
Regardless of reason or rhyme.

In the twilight's last gleam, let's discard the dream
That we cherished by dawn's early light,
For conquer we must, though our country goes bust,
We'll stand on our personal right.

So if anyone bothers to praise our forefathers
And recalls how they fought and they bled,
Just be glad they're not here to observe with a tear
Where the trails they once forged have now led.

1976

The Scar

This old scar? Oh, it isn't very much, —
A few more years and it will hardly show.
See, now, it scarcely quickens to the touch,
So well it healed. But do not probe below.
Sometimes it pains a little when the rain
With phantom footsteps trips along the eaves,
Or as I saunter down an April lane
And feel the spring-damp of last autumn's leaves.

I guess most all of us are marred in life,
And as for this, ah, well, —perhaps you know? —
A fall, a woman, or a flashing knife,
No matter now, it was so long ago …
Though even yet are nights I wonder why
When hearts are pierced, one does not always die?

A Thanksgiving Day Prayer

We thank Thee, Lord, for bringing us together
To enjoy this bounteous repast.
May the blessings that we ask of Thee
Be given also to those our loved ones
Who are absent from this table today.
As we partake of this meal,
Teach us also to savor
The other foods of life:
The joy of loved ones;
The richness of friendship;
The sweetness of sharing;
And the nourishment of little things,
For these, too, are the staff of life.
Teach us to plant
The seeds of our thoughts wisely
And cultivate our acts with care
So that the harvest
Will give us sustenance all our days.
Amen.

Jigsaw Puzzle

Only gradually does the pattern emerge ...
In the jumbled beginning the pieces seem to be
All of one shape,
All one design,
Yet each basking in its completeness,
Each like a play with characters and plot,
Bound in a fixed eternity.
One does not even think
To fit the pieces together,
For they are self-contained,
Like thoughts of home,
Or stars,
Or fields of wheat.
It's only later,
As one begins to analyze the game,
That one discerns the edges,
Cut unevenly,
No two alike,
And fashioned cunningly
To join with one another in a larger frame,
The one dependent on the others to give meaning.

At times there's hot debate concerning whether
The puzzle is first fashioned
In its entirety,
Like to a universe,
And then cut up,
Or if the parts are made
Quite independently. Some say
That thousands of them are stamped out,

Precise,
Identical,
To fit a multitude of self-same patterns.
But others think each piece
Is crafted with a loving skill,
Unmatched,
A revelation of unique identity
That in itself belies the supposition.
But no one knows for sure
Except the puzzle-maker,
And he is busy
Devising new pictures
For players yet to come.
At the very start it's hard to tell
The number of the pieces
And just how large the scene will grow to be.
The pieces in some boxes are so few,
So very few,
With horizons that encroach
Upon the view,
Knowingly or unknowingly, —
Better not to know.
Yet others for no apparent reason
Can boast a vast array
Of parts whose panoramic view
Seems to contain all humankind.
But then each box, —
Both those with parts too few
And those encompassing the larger scene —
Is quite complete when the last piece
Is placed upon the board.

It's here one wonders if
The puzzle is perchance one's own design,
To be constructed as one would,
Or if there ultimately is no choice
Of where and when and how and why
The parts comprise the whole.

The puzzle is its own excuse for being.
The game demands that one begin
Somewhere, —
Just where no one is sure it matters —
And so the first piece is selected
For a start, because of shape
Or size or circumstance,
No matter what,
The reason quite forgot
Before the final move.
The start may be in some far corner,
Remote and alien to the focus of the theme,
And what may seem the subject
Or the object of creation
May prove in retrospect
Incidental to the grand design.

As much by accident as purpose
A second piece joins with the first,
And then a third, all without conscious effort.
And slowly,
Almost imperceptibly,
One color fuses with the next
Of lighter or a darker hue,

And there appears to be the making of a pattern
Of a pleasant or disturbing mein,
Where faces, present, past and future
Build monuments to play and pain,
Frustration and exaltation,
A static tableau caught in time
In which both comic and the tragic muse
Go arm in arm.

Then for a little while, there is no need
To match the hills and rills
Made by the cutting. The picture of itself
Expands with graduated regularity
And dictates how the pieces fall in proper place,
Swiftly, ah, too swiftly,
As though ordained from time primordial
To be automatons to purposeful desire
Or else despite it.

The game is not all baubles and red roses.
At times the number of the pieces in itself,
Without a clue to how they fit
Into the total scheme,
Befogs the mind
And stretches at the axons.
And then the fact that they are strangers
Both to themselves and to the player
Makes for uncertainty and doubt.

And there are times the cutting or the figures,
Deceptive in their likeness,

Are mistaken for another piece
In time or place,
And those that seemed to mesh
In perfect harmony
Are not what they appeared to be
And do not fit the pattern.
And then again there is the wish,
Forever unfulfilled,
To probe beyond the limits of the game,
To saunter further down the trail
That stops abruptly
At the limits of the frame;
Or wish to know
The mind behind the face
So fixed with smile or frown;
Or wish again
Some distant view
Were central to the theme;
Or ultimate: to ponder why
This picture, after all,
And not another from the stock
The puzzle-maker distributes evenly,
One to each,
And never more than one.

And as the picture nears completion,
It's then, if ever, discovery is made
A piece or two is missing,
With only blankness where some face
Or place could spark delight.
Perhaps an oversight

In primal packaging,
One says,
While searching through the taunted mind
For more excuse than reason.

Most of the gaps are now filled in, —
Sometimes with pieces that amaze the eye—
But as the unplaced pieces dwindle down
One knows that those that still remain
Will not contain much great surprise.
And one can sense a pushing
Toward the boundaries, which,
If not as yet in view,
Are prescient in their presence.

The margins are the hardest part to finish.
They seem so much alike, and vary
Only to the practiced eye,
Grown weary of a game
That seeks repose in repetition.
In fact, the picture's now complete,
Except a final piece or two,
The hand reluctant to make further moves,
As though quiescence mothers immortality.

About this time one wonders
What may be the purpose of the game.
A vital urge for action may well play a part.
More likely though the reason is
To solve the puzzle and to see
The picture in totality, a quest

That wonderment repays in coin
That's true or false, —
Depending on the point of view —
Unless it's all a show
Put on to entertain the puzzle-maker
In an idle hour.

And now one's tempted,
Just before the final piece is laid in place,
To throw up the game
And scramble all the pieces,
To start afresh for what it's worth,
With hope to change, enlarge the scene,
New monuments to build,
New names to join
The old familiar faces.
But those who've tried this
Tell the rest that scramble it
And start afresh
As many times as there are pieces,
The picture will not change,
But will remain
With all its beauty and its pain,
Frozen in its joy and sorrow,
Caught now and forevermore
In graven grooves the jigsaw makes
Before the box is neatly stored away
On some forgotten, dusty shelf
In the closet of
All yesterdays.

Last Leaf

Outside my window hanging high
And dark against an azure sky
A single tree-bound leaf remains,
Despite past snows and spring-borne rains
And winds that swept the branches bare
But left this one leaf dangling there
To greet the April buds as they
Renew the cyclic counterplay
Of birth and growth, maturity,
And then decay's obscurity.

And watching thus, I seek its mood:
Does it deplore its solitude,
Lamenting in a feckless way
The golden glow of yesterday
When all was greening, life imbued
With youth and hope and certitude,
Comparing past and present in
The maze of all that might have been,
Decrying molds in which were cast
The fortunes of the long-gone past,
Belike a prophet or a sage,
A symbol of another age?

Or does it glory in the chance
That some benignant circumstance
Has proffered it to briefly mime
The sweet redundancy of time,
A spur, a budding progeny
That through recurring alchemy

Transmutes old dreams yet unfulfilled
To new-found heights on which to build,
And, by example, mute but clear,
Providing hope, destroying fear,
Give strength to those who by decree
Must live in nature's mystery?

On Listening to Burton's "Ariel" Symphony

I

The girl said, "Oh, what beauty
Shining through the darkest nights
Of torment and despair!" Her cry
Was not of self but of the universal heart.
And this the composition caught:
The harmonies so wrought
To move celestial spheres
In proper orbit did the artist
And the poet have their way
And world were of their making.

Like to a falling star
She burned a blue and lovely light—
Intense illumination amplified
Within the earthly atmosphere
Until the brilliant radiance,
Exhausted by the friction of our time,
Burned out, fragmented by
The world of men and deeds,
The flower choked by all the weeds.

And this the music understood
And magnified and clothed her words
In dress most suited to her mood,
So that I saw her in the varied hues,
Her gown now white in purity,
The blood-red in a fevered cry,
Then in the ink-pitch blackness
Of a shroud. Yet through it all

The magic of her song entwined
With what the music wrought
So that I glimpsed within the lined
Interstices the beauty heart and soul combined.

II

The boy said, "Her old man
Held much too tight a rein
And left her hobbled in the mind.
He choked her off
Before she learned to breathe.
I guess you'd call her in some way
A mixed-up kid,
A crazy quilt of brain waves,
The somber patterns almost lost to view.

"The music and the words she wrote,
They turned me off and on,
Like traffic lights attached to every pore,
So what I understood I liked,
And what I didn't like,
I didn't understand,
Or is it just the other way about?
Maybe that's the answer to
A lot of problems that we have today.

"She sounded like someone who climbed
The tallest peaks only to find
The air so rarified

That all she saw spread out below
Was out of focus, too distorted to
Distinguish vision from reality,
So that the meaning of her words
And of the music, too, was just beyond
Whatever makes us tick in time
With all the clocks that regulate our lives."

III

The woman said, "The poetry that she conceived
Was like a child, so innocent,
Naive, and yet as old and wise
As that of ancients
Crawling out of hoary caves—
Gushing forth from wells of wisdom
Deep within a breast full laden
With an earth-lode's woe,
Its voice a poignant protest
To a deaf and cloud-packed sky.
And yet her words were lifted up on high
Exultantly, above the song
And yet a part of it
So that the two conjoined in bold experiments
Of such originality they bridged
The past and present forms
To send wild tremors to
The future world of creativity.

"The harmony she lacked the music gave
To violins, bestowing beauty to
The meaning of the words,
And sent the senses reeling for release
From grief too great for word or thought
With all that's lovely brought to naught."

IV

The man said, "It's much too soon
To judge the lasting merit of this work.
The distillation of the years
May find it breaks new ground
For progeny to emulate.
Or it may be they'll put it on the shelf
Of aspiration not achieved,
Where it will sit collecting dust
And only played on odd occasion when
Some learned hands decide to illustrate
Abortive flights of striving past.

"Perhaps I did not catch
The import of the verse, if not the song.
To me the mushroomed clouds
Of death and dark despond
So much outweighed the fairy flakes
Of light, that if some form of Ariel
I saw and heard, it was his alter ego
In whom the watch-springs of his mind,
Like hers, were wound too tight

To face the morning light.
She had no tolerance for pain,
And thus was wracked when birds' eggs fell
From nests a thousand miles away.
I find no way to tune myself
To wave lengths of discordant minds
And music in which they're embalmed.
And so it is the scales of judgment hang
Between the valiant striving for the goal
And all the turbulence of churning souls,
So that I wonder if the verses mark
A spark of stark originality
Or static fragments from an uncoiled brain,
With music on some sonic level
That touches evenly both God and devil."

October 26, 1976

Handprints

Handprints on once spotless walls,
Marks of crayons, bouncing balls;
Scattered playthings own the floor,
Dolls and cut-outs by the score.

Ghosts of food on linen white,
Heirloom treasures out of sight;
Gurgling sounds replacing talk,
A playpen where we used to walk.

Firm, demanding, then it seems,
Coy, seductive, lost in dreams;
Exasperating, yet adored,
Aspiration's great reward.

Pratfalls, scratches, causing fright,
Walking floors through the night;
Sturdy, fragile, tiny tot,
Object of creation's plot.

All-pervasive symbol of
Cherished, priceless, radiant love;
With troubles, fears repaid in style
When Meredith bequeaths a smile.

December 1976

Friendship

The ties that bind
Grow taut about the liquid heart,
Squeezing tiny drops of caring
Into pools of lasting trust.
And these in turn form rivulets
Of affection
That seek outlet,
Converging into streams
Of outpouring love.

The pools are formed
By a multitude of happenings,
Drop-like incidents,
Each one too small perhaps
To more than moisten
The absorptive heart,
But large enough in aggregate
To saturate all being.

And this is called friendship.

1977

The Mountain Trail

We have climbed the mountain trail
Together, hand in hand,
With ready arms outstretched
To aid and guide the other
When the trail grew steep,
When the footing threatened,
When the underbrush of life
Obscured the path of living.
And we have looked on beauty
From the vantage point of summits,
Found new perspective from the view
Of sights and insights shared,
And gloried in the distant range
As in the tiny bud that, half concealed,
Peeped out from some neglected cranny,
And found the beauty and the glory
Sublimated in the sharing.
And I have found in you
Devotion, love, and courage, too,
That smoothed the rock-strewn trail,
That lulled the whipping winds,
And made a golden harvest of the years
As we, together, share the mountain trail.

Words

Words:
Status symbols of the higher mammal;
The yardstick of man's progress;
The heritage of all things past;
Calling cards of the educated tongue;
The tools of fools and poets;
Society's substitute for muscle;
Exhaust valves of the tension machine;
A requiem to past mistakes;
Balm for the suffering heart;
A banquet for the questing mind;
Peepholes to the soul;
Survival's last persuader:
        These are the mark of man
        And men,
        What makes man more than beast
        Or less:
Words.

        Some words are clothes,
In and out of fashion,
Hiding or revealing
The mind's anatomy,
Cloaking its design
Or baring it, stark and gaunt.
        Some are finely woven words
That speak of quality,
Spun upon a loom of thought
With pride of craft,
Displaying the rich fabric of the mind.

Some are tinsel-shiny words,
Rhinestones to the ear,
Ornaments to wear
Attracting those
Who buy a bauble for a gem.
And some are safe and proven words,
Society's nether garment,
Slipped on to protect the wearer,
Or to escape from thought,
Labels on the suit of custom
About which no question will be asked
And answers never needed.

A thousand thousand words
To right a wrong
Or wrong a right;
To blunt the blow
Or strike it;
To quicken the pulse
Or soothe the senses;
To shadow resolve
Or illuminate.

Clean enduring words
That march steadfast
Down the corridors of time
And have the ring of verity;
Treasured, priceless words
That warm a heart
And whose reflected glow
Warms him who utters them;

Words like swords of steel,
Sheathed by the mind,
Which, once wielded, have an edge
To cut the strongest ties;
Dresden words, of cup-like lustre rare,
Hand-wrought and used with loving care
To spread a feast of thought
Upon the patterned damask of the mind;
Hand-clasped wordless tongue
And pour forth all
That voice cannot express;
Squandered words that have no worth
Beyond the user's use;
New-found words,
Quaffed half hesitantly,
Explored with fresh delight,
Then sipped and rolled about the tongue, —
Rare vintage to the jaded taste.

Words that have a special meaning
Known to very few,
Conjured out of some occasion
Covered by the tracks of time,
And yet the word still lingers
And binds these very few
In some warm glow
That they unspoken
Will cherish till they die;

Words that bubble fountain-like
Up and down the throat
And burst upon the lips
In an extravagance of idea flow;
Words that slip like ghouls
Quite suddenly from out unguarded lips,
And now must haunt forever
The graveyard of regret;
Words that climb the stairway of the soul,
Linking heart and mind and spirit, too,
In ways ineffable,
Expressing that which cannot be expressed,
Bringing understanding to that which
Cannot be understood,
Aspiring to the higher stars
That twinkle indistinct
Beyond the reaches of the tongue or mind.
Words....

The Pebbled Ridge

She heard the key within the lock and heard
Him call her name, a ritual that they
Had practiced down the years. She answered and
With quickened step moved toward his open arms.
He kissed her brow, just as he always had
So many times before. She would have asked
The questions that one does about his day
But something in his manner held her tongue.

And when they ate, discussion of the day's
Events was not forthcoming till he cleared
His throat — a signal in itself — and said
Offhand, "They offered me the job today."
She gave no sign that she had heard except
Her spoon's arc in the air had paused within
Her hand half imperceptibly before
Resuming its accustomed course. There was
No need for explanation any more.

She knew who "they" were and could picture them
Around the long green table of the room
That featured portraits of past Chairmen of
The Board, just as she knew without a word
The job they offered was the topmost goal
Of all their striving down the toilful years.
Why do the years provide the largesse when
The need is gone? She blinked away the thoughts
Of sacrifice that they had gladly made
So that the children's path would be so much
Less arduous than theirs. For years too long

To count he'd climbed the ladder that they call
Success. And now the topmost rung of all
Was his for just the grasp, the rung that he
Had never striven for, as such, and yet
Deserved. She vainly sought his eyes and felt
The weight of silence that enveloped them.

And willingly she let these thoughts suffuse
Her mind and run like tiny rivulets into
Each cranny of her consciousness in hope
That they would drown the apprehension that,
Like bubbles in fermenting wine, rose round
The edges of her reminiscences,
Beclouding all the beauty of his news
And leaving on her mental tongue a taste
Of bitterness that would not be denied.

Within her she felt no joy, no surge
Of jubilation that was rightly theirs.
A wisp of smile that fled before it broke
Upon her face betokened that she plumbed
The fateful irony of all that was
And all that they could ever hope to gain.
Then finally she asked the question that
They both knew must be asked: "And what of Jim?"
And knew the answer long before he spoke.
Again she sought his eyes, but they were on
His empty plate, as though it gave to him
Asylum from the thoughts they both now shared.
He found his voice: "They think he's grown too old

To run the show, that with a younger hand
Up at the top—a more elastic mind—
We'd gain back those accounts we've lost, and win
A wider market with the new ideas
That I've been recommending all these years."
A furtive glance and then his eyes escaped
To focus back upon the plate.

She gave
No sign but asked again in voice the same
As she had asked before, "And what of Jim?"
He heaved a sigh. "They think he might retire
Or that some honorary post be made
To offer him. You know he's not been well.
I'm not sure that he even knows as yet
The sudden action that they took today.
His illness kept him from the meeting and
I'm not the one to tell him what they've done."

In voice too casual for the words' import
She asked, "And did you tell them you'd accept?"
He answered quickly as if to escape
The turmoil that infused his mind. "I said
I'd let them know my answer in three days.
They're anxious to get on. They know just how
I feel about old Jim, but if I don't
Accept, the chances are they'll look
About for someone else to fill the post.
One thing is sure: I'll have no second chance."
"He always was and is your friend," she said,

"And seems more like a father to us both
Than just a kindly boss." Her thoughts again
Receded to the days long gone when Jim
Had offered him the work they needed to
Survive, and how Jim helped them when they bought
Their home, and how, when illness struck their son—
The boy they named for Jim—he saw to it
He had the best of care regardless of
The cost.

And he, as though divining what
Was in her mind, was quick to counter-thrust.
"We paid him back to the last cent," he said,
"And what is more, the work I've done for all
Of them enabled him to point with pride
To his accomplishments. He cannot say
I haven't been his friend. His voice was edged
As though the sharpness of his tone would cut
The ties with which his heart entwined his mind.

"And what is friendship?" Now her voice was soft,
Too soft, he thought, and knowing her so well,
He felt her pain commingle with his own.
He eyed the plate once more as though to find
Response beyond the hackneyed words that came
To mind. "Oh, friendship is the close-knit bond
That holds two people in its clasp without
Regard for what they say or do." He moved
Uneasily upon the chair and set
His jaw as men are sometimes wont to do
When words that seek to conquer fail their task.

Her head inclined to nod, and when she spoke
He strained to catch the words he feared to hear.
"There is no gift more precious than the one
That friendship gives, nor any treasure locked
In vaults can ransom it when gone.
To me it is a golden thread of trust
That twines about the mind, brocading joy,
Repairing wounded hearts, and tinting with
Its glow the tinseled tapestry of time."

They left the table as it was and sought
Without a further word the spot where they
So many times before had gone to seek
The answers to the problems of the past.
He took her hand, so soft it seemed, to guide
Her down the pebbled path that led into
The garden plot. Her palm gave off a warmth
That surged through him as though they both were one.
And slow she moved her eyes about as though
In way ineffable to call back from
A dusty store of memories the time
He labored to perfect the winding trail
When love was young so very long ago.

They sat together on the garden bench,
Just so the sun and overhanging leaves
Could join together in a dappled dance
Upon the features of her upturned face.
He watched this interplay of sun and shade,
Of light and dark, upon her still smooth brow

And marveled how it caught the beauty of
Her countenance and yet enlarged somehow
The struggle that enmeshed the two of them
Within a net of conflict that destroyed
The harmony that had been theirs, the surge
Of quick elation he had carried home.

She watched a canopy of clouds provide
A curtain for the setting sun, that shot
A host of rays of vari-colored hues
Above the clouds and up the western sky
As though proclaiming one last tribute to
The dying day, then turned her head aside
So as to better see the outline of
The face she loved, now deeply graven by
The darkening shadows as they stole across
The sward. Then night, as if impatient at
Delay, attacked the color of the trees,
Once etched, now blurred beyond identity.

A bird came by to perch upon a limb
And sang a threnody to parting day.
And in her thoughts she envied it a life
So free from judgments faced by man.
We all are prisoners, she mused, of minds
Creating discord in the song of life,
And are so structured that the more we try
To finely tune the keyboard of the brain
The greater is the dissonance we make.
And when she spoke, it was as though he heard

A stranger's voice, half muted yet so strong:
"The answer is, I know, for you to make,
But I should hate to rouse up in the night
And find you still aware."

His sole response
Was with a foot that pushed the pebbles to
A ridge that left a shallow in the path.
And this small ridge he magnified until
He saw it as a wall that rose so high
It seemed to dwarf them on each side of it.
How long he gazed he did not know: there is
No measurement of time to register
The heartbeat of the soul's eternities.

And she could feel within herself the taut
Vibrations of a bow, so tightly strung
A quiver's touch would break, and sensed
The silent struggle that enveloped him.

They spoke no word, and only twice he stirred,
The first to smooth the pebbled ridge he'd made,
Done so with care and such decisiveness
She wondered at the act's finality.
And this complete, he found a sudden calm,
And all the tensive pressures disappeared,
As if he had been freed from inner chains
That bound his chest, and left his mind at peace,
Unfettered in a sweet serenity
That gloried in the wisdom that was hers.

The other time a bell, insistent in
Its ring, had summoned him within the house.
And with him gone so long, she sat and watched
A panoply of coruscating stars
Appear above the moon to guide its path
Like street lights of the sky. And she found in
The sight a wish the stars that guided them
Would light their proper course. And thus she sat,
Her mind divided in its troubled thoughts,
Part worshiping the wonder of the night
And part despairing of their anguished plight.
She vaguely caught the fragrance of the blooms
That nodded close at hand as if they sought
To give some perfumed solace to her pain.
Her glance fell on the spot where once the ridge
Had been, and she recalled the care he took
In mending what his foot had done. Could this
Small mound, she wondered, symbolize a goal
That his ambition spurred him to, a goal
Now caught in circumstance too delicate
For ledger sheet of gain or loss? Or was
This but a fancied figment of her mind,
And all the ridge exemplified was just
A gesture when the heart is sore beset?
Or—sudden thought—had he seen in their plight
A barrier to blight their past and all
The future had to give, so that they'd face
A gulf between them in the years to come?

But then the smoothness of the pebbled path
Recalled his act and hope surged through her frame,
A hope that brought conviction to her mind.
And in her heart she knew his answer now.

When he returned and sat again, she moved
Close by as though her strength was his to take.
Her hand reached up to him and soft caressed
His burnished cheek, intent to smooth the lines
That heedless time, like tumbling streams unchecked,
Cascading down the mordant spendthrift years,
Had eroded the once trackless sheen.
Her gesture was so slight it seemed, and yet
To him it proffered all the love that one
Can give. He marveled that it cost her not
A word, and yet it gave her all to him.
And he, his spirits kindled in the glow
Assurance radiates, retrieved her hand
In his and brought down to that clasp his lips
To seal the motion in a silent vow
Of affirmation in their steadfast trust.
When finally he spoke, his voice was far
Away. "At times it seems it's hard to see
The road that's straight ahead." He paused and when
He spoke again his voice was no more strained:
"I'm thankful that I have my compass by
My side."
            She looked off to the stars and saw
They'd never been so bright. "Sometimes," she said,
"The heart's a better compass than the mind."

He nodded absently before he spoke:
"Jim called to say he'd learned the action of
The Board. He's not without his friends. He sensed
The quandary I was in and urged me to
Accept. He said if I would take the job,
He wouldn't fight to save it for himself."
He looked down to her face and smiled, and now
His eyes were full upon her own. "I told
Him I had long enjoyed the battles that
We fought together, side by side, and saw
No reason why I now should change my stand."
She bent down low and softly stroked the path.
Then filled with all the radiance the night
Had given them, she took his hand in hers
And led him slowly back into the house.

Boundary Brook

The walk down to the brook is far enough.
It isn't that the going grows so rough
Or that the neighbors care if I keep on,
Ignoring map lines like the doe at dawn,
But there is something in the feel of earth
Beneath the feet that is one's own, a worth
Quite undefined, that sparks an inner glow
That's not the same as pride. The dogs, they know.

The garden patch comes first, and then the field,
Before the copse provides sufficient shield
To hide from view both birds and brook, —combined
Asylum, too, for creatures of the mind.
I like it best perhaps at first spring thaw,
When rushing waters, freed from winter's maw,
Boil up and foam about the stubborn rocks
And sing of freedom from restraint that mocks
The strictures man and matter would provide
Against the flow of nature's youthful tide.

No matter now. It's autumn and the brook
Has long since lost its bold aggressive look.
The wild exultant cry of fledgling spring
Is now reduced to rill-lapped murmuring,
And placid waters tend to magnify
The mirrored stillness of the mindless sky,
As though the pulse of time itself were slowed
When nature, too, is wearied of its load.
Reluctantly I leave before I would,
For dusk is filling up the darkling wood.

Handprints Four

Shortly winged time provides
Fresh new handprints on all sides;
Toys for two now own the floor,
All there were and many more.

Voices now are heard in pairs,
Each demanding equal shares;
Questions raised in unison,
Require response by Solomon!

Doubled problems, doubled fears,
Doubled love as each endears.
Twice the labor, twice the pain,
Twice the sunshine after rain.

With Meredith the teacher now,
While Kate as pupil makes her bow,
The two bestowing as a team
Boundless love and joy supreme.

1979

The Wreck of the Nancy Lee

'Twas barely dawn in 'Frisco town,
As foggy as can be,
With just a few men at the wharf
When we put out to sea.

That day we watched the shore recede
And blend into the blue;
Then there was naught but the ship's wake
And gulls to charm the crew.

The captain's orders read to sail
Straight out across the bay
And set a course, let come what will,
For faraway Cathay.

That day the gulls deserted us
And fled back to the shore;
Too late I wished to fly with them
To where I'd been before.

The ship was an old barkentine
And named the Nancy Lee;
From Nantucket to Macao
It plied the western sea.

The hold was filled with cotton goods
And looms and guns as well,
And if they stored some opium,
No one on board would tell.

The captain was a decent man
And wore a square cut beard.
The men who took pride in their work
Had nothing to be feared.

The first mate loved to spin a yarn
Of men and ships he knew;
The tales he told were full of gore
And some perhaps were true.

The second mate was all for work:
Excuse he'd not condone.
When others gathered, watches done,
He found himself alone.

The third mate was a jolly sort,
A black patch on one eye.
The knife was all he seemed to fear;
No need to wonder why.

The bosun was an ugly man,
His face both pocked and scarred,
And something in his look betold
Not just his face was marred.

The crew was of a motley sort,
Their dress peculiar, too,
And as for all the tongues they spoke,
I recognized but two.

I was the only passenger;
I hoped to see and learn
And write about the Orient
Upon my safe return.

With sails that billowed in the breeze,
We ploughed the swelling sea,
The ship's bell tolling off each watch
With dull monotony.

The only sounds that could be heard
Were of the winch's groan,
The idle talk, the flapping sails,
The wind's protesting moan.

Each day a copper sun arose
And arched across the sky;
Each night the stars blinked down on us
And traced their paths on high.

It seemed the elements all knew
Their course above the sea,
While we below just sailed and sailed
Like in eternity.

One day some porpoises appeared
And frolicked off the stern;
We fed them till they had their fill
And left not to return.

One night the deep was strangely filled
With phosphorescent eyes.
It made us feel the more alone,
Although 'twas otherwise.

The crewmen had a deck of cards
To wile the time away.
I would not join, but saw no harm
In watching them at play.

But soon the bosun was accused
Of cheating, then a fight.
The bosun had no friends aboard:
They buried him that night.

A Portagee they put in irons
And in the brig was cast.
I wondered if they freed him when
The ship had seen its last.

Both sea and days slipped slowly by,
Devoid of shallows, peaks.
The captain's Sabbath prayer was
The way we marked the weeks.

We boxed the compass with our gaze
And found a great void there,
Except the blue sky overhead
And water everywhere.

The rats infested the ship's hold
And as the days rolled by,
Their hunger brought them to the deck
To all the crew defy.

One of their kind my cabin found;
I fed him as a whim,
The two of us grew quite attached;
I even talked to him.

But then one day the order came
To poison all they could,
And soon I missed my visitor,
For he was gone for good.

The carpenter's accordion
Was sweet to ev'ry ear;
The third mate in a deep rich voice
Provided notes to cheer.

One night they played a sad sea song—
The chorus we'd all sing—
And down the years I sing it yet,
'Tis worth remembering:

"The sea's a sweet and lovely lass
When she decides to be;
The very sight of her brings joy
And sighs of ecstasy."

"But never, never trust the sea,
Though she may seem your friend;
For she'll betray you soon or late,
Destroy you in the end."

"She's like a warm and loving bride
With rapturous embrace;
A radiant and soothing wife,
Endowed with charm and grace."

"But never, never trust the sea,
Though she may seem your friend;
For she'll betray you soon or late,
Destroy you in the end."

"For she's a fickle mistress who
Will seek your heart to win,
And having won, destroys your soul, —
As treacherous as sin."

"So never, never trust the sea,
Though she may seem your friend;
For she'll betray you soon or late,
Destroy you in the end."

"Yes, she's a cruel, ruthless queen
With malice in her womb;
She'll raise you up with blandishments,
Then toss you to your doom."

"So never, never trust the sea,
Though she may seem your friend;
For she'll betray you soon or late,
Destroy you in the end."

"Best close your heart and list not to
Her siren melody;
She'll woo you to dispatch you
If you put out to sea."

"So never, never trust the sea,
Though she may seem your friend;
For she'll betray you soon or late,
Destroy you in the end."

And then there came long days of drought
And overbearing heat;
The sun it scorched the decks and men
And spoiled the salted meat.

And as the days turned into weeks,
The sun still shone so strong.
The wind was hot, the men in turn
Made much of fancied wrong.

They grumbled at their daily work,
The meat, they cried, was bad,
The water rations all too small,
But it was all we had.

They thought the crowded fo'c'sle was
By far too hot for sleep;
They itched of lice and bedbug bites,
Their clothes were all acreep.

Their discontent was centered in
A group of Portagee
Who thought the bosun's death was just,
And sought their friend to free.

The men responded to commands
Without alacrity;
The officers wore sidearms now,
Ostentatiously.

But though the captain did his best
To bring about accord,
The second mate said openly
He'd throw them overboard.

I spent the time much by myself
In cabined sanctity,
And found a stout belaying pin
To take to bed with me.

The outcome of this parlous plight
No one will ever know,
For what may seem of great import
May not be always so.

The drought, the heat, the tainted food,
The water and the plot,
Were changed by sudden circumstance
And grievances forgot.

For then one day the wind dropped down;
It caused a deathly still,
Nor any canvas on the ship
Did any breezes fill.

I sought the captain on the bridge;
His greeting was most grave.
He said he couldn't fathom why
The glass should so behave.

He 'lowed as how the pressure was
As low as he had seen
In all his years before the mast; —
Its cause he could not glean.

But then the weather thickened;
The sun was lost from sight.
Great drops of rain began to fall;
It grew as dark as night.

The captain had all hands on deck;
The first mate checked the hold;
The second mate harangued the crew;
The third mate's smile grew cold.

Then one by one they furled the sails,
The large ones and the small,
The booms and spars were made secure;
We did not move at all.

They stowed the gear they didn't need,
Made snug each port and catch,
Turned down the wicks on ev'ry lamp,
And battened ev'ry hatch.

The cargo was distributed,
The ballast made secure;
The ship seemed set to ride the storm
And any threat endure.

The breeze then freshened to a wind,
The wind became a gale,
I leaned against it for support
And grabbed the poopdeck rail.

A crewman started in to sing
The old familiar hymn,
But in the howling of the gale
His voice was mighty dim.

And soon the sea became awake
With billows cresting high
To break across the plunging bow
As though it was the sky.

Each time we plunged between the waves
I thought 'twould be the last;
Each time we rose I breathed a sigh,
But watched the highest mast.

The ship would rise high by the bow,
Then drop into a trough,
Then shudder up from stem to stern,
Bedecked with spume and froth.

The first mate thought about his wife,
The second of the shore,
The third mate thought of both of these
And of a laughing whore.

The cook cross-legged the galley deck,
His mind in Buddhist dreams;
The carpenter kneeled down to pray
But eyed the vessel's seams.

The cabin boy with thoughts of home
Bit hard his trembling lip.
The captain had no thoughts but one:
The safety of his ship.

The royal mast was first to go,
Top gallant mast was next.
A crewman tried his best to pray
But soon forgot the text.

They lashed the steersman to the wheel,
But soon he made no sound.
The captain sought him out himself
And found the creature drowned.

A yardarm from the mizzen sheet
Crashed down and hit the deck.
Too late a seaman saw it come;
It broke the poor man's neck.

The wind picked up a forward sail—
It was the flying jib—
And threw it back upon the ship
To crack the first mate's rib.

The second mate gave a command;
The men did not obey.
He started forward in a rage;
A wave washed him away.

The third mate got entangled in
Lines from the aftermast,
And when it toppled in the sea
I knew he'd breathed his last.

The crew that once the yards had swarmed
Now numbered but a few
And in their distraught state were torn
As to what best to do.

They sought the safety of the hold,
Yet feared to stay below.
They feared the hold, they feared the deck,
There was no place to go.

I felt a pounding in my heart
That nothing would abate;
It seemed like knocking at life's door
Done by the fist of fate.

Then for a time the wind died down,
I felt a hopeful thrill,
And though the waters raged no less,
The wind was strangely still.

But soon the gale picked up in force,
But from another lie.
The hurricane blew in reverse;
We'd passed the tempest's eye.

The three main masts had held up well,
But now they felt the strain;
Those fore and aft both split in two;
Our fate was now quite plain.

The mainmast was the last to go.
It made a fearful boom,
Like all the thunder down the years
Proclaiming thus our doom.

And with it fell the staysails,
And all the mainsheets, too,
The clewlines, bowlines, tackle, block,
Enmeshing half the crew.

It fell athwart the cluttered deck,
Amidships, beam to beam,
Half on the deck, half in the sea,
It was the devil's dream.

The captain swore a mighty oath,
God-fearing though he was.
Few men in such extremity
Are not without their flaws.

I felt the vessel shudder like
'Twas in the devil's grip,
And heard the captain give one cry:
"All hands abandon ship!"

The men swung out the three ship boats—
The others had been lost—
To launch them in the frightful sea
Would be at frightful cost.

The first was shattered by a mast,
The second one capsized,
The third broke loose and washed away
Before they realized.

The stern was first to be awash,
And then it disappeared;
The bow rose up against the sky,
A fearful sight and weird.

I grabbed a spar and stood transfixed,
The water at my waist.
A tow'ring wave then lifted me:
My destiny I faced.

The waves they grabbed my arms and legs,
They tugged at ev'ry part
As though they were an octopus
Now sucking at my heart.

I felt myself pulled down and down;
My senses lost their touch.
I was a chip the vortex tossed
Within the maelstrom's clutch.

And then, with lungs about to burst,
I suddenly was shot
Up to the surface of the sea
By forces I knew not.

I gasped for air, my senses cleared,
The spar still in my grip;
Unknowingly I'd held it tight
Since I had left the ship.

I rose atop a mighty wave
And saw the ship close by;
The captain stood upon the bridge:
He was prepared to die.

A moment there he stood transfixed,
Majestic and alone.
A wave engulfed the ship and him, —
I stared but both were gone.

The waves still sucked my shaken frame
And tossed me to and fro.
I wished to live, I wished to die,
I wished to end my woe.

Then quickly as it had begun
The storm did then abate.
The wind and rain passed to the east,
But it was far too late.

I searched for captain, mates and crew,
I scanned the boundless sea;
In all the waters round about
There was no one but me.

I searched for sail, I searched the sky, —
At times my mind grew odd —
I searched the conscience of my past,
And, yes, I searched for God.

I thought of mother, father, home,
And of a winsome maid,
But more I thought of sharks and such,
And closed my eyes and prayed.

One does not think coherently
In sorry circumstance;
The thoughts flick in and out the brain
Like cards one deals by chance.

I rested on the spar that day,
At night upon my back;
My eyes swelled up, my throat grew parched,
My skin began to crack.

I swam, I dozed, I swam again,
The spar beneath my chin.
I feared the day, I feared the night,
I feared a dorsal fin.

How long the water's fluid grip
Held me I do not know.
A moment is eternity
For those who suffer so.

But then with dawn I saw a ship
And madly waved my arm.
It gave no sign that I could spy,
Which filled me with alarm.

I shouted through the elements:
My God, can they be blind?
And then again I ceased to care,
My thoughts composed, resigned.

A longboat came to succor me;
I could not help but weep.
I thanked my God to thus be spared
The perils of the deep.

The trip to shore was quickly made,
And then a voyage home.
I made a vow right there to stay
And nevermore to roam.

But now and then I raise a glass
And toast the Nancy Lee
And all the brave and gallant men
Who with her put to sea.

OUTRACE THE DAWN

From 1980 to 1989

Grace

We thank Thee, Lord, that you have sent
This friend to us today
May he share in the happiness
That he has brought our way.

And may Thy hand guide and protect
And comfort him always
And may our love and friendship stand
Steadfast all our days.

1980

Hook, Line and Sinker

Invite him for lunch
Without stating your mission
That you're baiting your hook
On a fishing expedition.

Invite him for dinner
With candles and wine.
Perish the thought
That you're casting your line.

Invite him for breakfast
And if you've been wise,
He's swallowed the hook,
Now just reel in the prize.

Last Respects

I hope there'll be some laughter
When my ship puts out to sea,
And may you have a drink or two, —
The second one's for me.

And may you see some faces of
Old friends almost forgot,
And sit and reminisce a bit—
I'd like that part a lot.

I'd like to say a "thank you"
To every one you see
For friendship lasting through the years
And for all you've done for me.

And if my name is mentioned,
And remembered as one does,
I hope it's as I'd like to be
And not the way I was.

On Reading Kristen's Poems

Comes a note in a bottle
Cast up from the sea —
The sea those you love
Still cherish because
In the seaweed and sand
And the smell of the salt
They, too, built their castles
That survived time and tide
And helped them to answer
The questions each ponders.

So you in your quest
For an answer to dreams
That enchant as they vanish,
And turmoiled illusions
That tease, plague, and nourish
All hearts that float free,
Find answers emerging,
Pointing up to the sky
Like the castles of sand
One builds in youth's climbing, —
Find answers, half-formed,
Deep in self,
Self enriching,
That with tongue that is silver
Breast waves to respond
In a way you alone
Can find truth beyond answers:

Priceless gift caught
In the net of youth's trawling,
Sheer beauty discovered
To guard like a pearl
And to mold and develop
In substance and form
Into treasures to share
With those who would listen
For the chime of a bell
Through the roar of life's ocean.

January 1986

the moon's not a balloon

cry down the echo chambers
of soundless time
and with fingernails
gnawed
        to the moons
climb the layered stalagmites
of golden memory
seeking purchase
        (ah! repurchase!)
of magic moments
priceless beyond price,
frozen in the security
of a yesterday made eternal
if only
      one
        could
              obliterate
the here and now.

This Day

This day—
This precious day—
This here and now,
A droplet in the flow of time,
Yet child of all that was before:
The scion of all yesterdays,
Compressed in microcosmic art
For all of humankind
To savor and to cherish,
Discover and explore,
From deep abyss to highest star …

This day—
This unique day—
This banquet for the mind
And body and the soul,
The essence of all being,
Creator of tomorrow's plot,
Ancestor of what is to be,
So swiftly gone
Yet linked eternally
Within the chain of destiny …

This day—
This pristine day—
Inchoate, formless at its birth,
To fashion as we will
Into a rebus of new hopes,
New dreams, new starts, new ways
To shape the future's course

for each to mold as best he may
Within the matrix of tomorrow's clay...
This day.

Handprints Six

Two sets of handprints suddenly
Grown now to three by love's decree,
And two young ladies find with pride
A tiny toddler by their side.

What magic does this mite provide
To gain attention far and wide,
With wishes not to be denied
That keep all guardians occupied?

His character a recipe
Of brains, good nature—heaps of glee—
Large scoops of charm, so often pert,
Determination for dessert.

So quick to climb, so quick to smile,
So quick to capture hearts the while,
Conveying wishes in a tone
That forms a language all his own.

With Meredith and Kate a pair
To mold, to teach, to guide, to share
The dream of happiness this tot
Has brought to all who call him Scott.

December 1987

Les Roses du Septembre

The rosebuds one discovers in September
Are first to feel the finger of the frost,
And he who's touched the doorstep of December
Must find content in scents of blooms long lost.

For rosebuds, like romance, each has its season,
And neither boasts of immortality,
Except an essence, clinging beyond reason,
To always be enshrined in memory.

Five Mile Beach

I

As far as eye can see and far beyond
The beach unfolds before the lifted eye,
And where we walk close by the water's edge,
The sand is hard and firm,
Packed down by restless tides,
As though the sea itself
In elemental guilt
Would wash away all vestiges
Of deeds long done,
Of deeds it wishes to forget.

Farthest from the ocean side
The sand is loose and soft,
Yielding to the sandcrab's busy feet,
Unmolded by the sea or man,
With many tiny, smooth-edged mounds,
Gravestones of ten thousand angry winds
That came and spent their rage so long ago.

Between the hard sand and the soft
There is a line that marks the tidal reach,
A line that staggers drunkenly
Along the beach
Dissolving in a blur of nothingness.
When wild-eyed fancy spreads her wings,
I like to think this line
Is presentness, the here and now,
And that the sands on either side

Are past and future of all time;
The firm hard sand the past so quick forgot,
Obliterated by the guileful tides;
The soft sand inchoate and unformed,
With challenges of years to come,
Amorphous clay to mold the future role of life,
Undecipherable,
Each grain encompassing
Millennia of all that is to be.

But this is whimsical to such degree
I do not speak of it, but let it pass,
Lost like the dreams of those
Who walked the beach in time long gone …
Who walked the beach so long before …

It was so many years ago, and yet
One almost sees them now, again.
A group of them there were,
Scarce more than boys, with scratchy stubble
On their chins, found only in those
Yet too young or much too old to care.
Perhaps it was a picnic organized
At harvest time, with pretty girls
And cider close at hand,
And baskets filled with ripened fruit
And meats rotating on a spit.
And there were games and frolics that
Sweet youth alone can justify.
Or then perhaps it was a winter's dance,

Put on to break the shut-in boredom of the snow
Piled high outside the door,
The laughter of the girls
In counterpoint to fiddles' lively tunes.

In either case there were the jokes
And banter all about,
And shouts of laughter in the air,
For life is green and gold with promises
When pulses quicken to the beat of youth.

There was a lull in the festivities—
'Twas then that someone said
The mate was looking for recruits
To man the stations in the boat
Down there by the Light,
The new longboat, swinging on its davits,
High above the reaches of the tides.

Then brags and boasts
Mix with the banter's tune,
And dares are quickly made
And just as quickly pledged.
The presence of the girls
Is like a spur:
Excited squeals and cautionary fears
Work equally to egg the daring on.
And more: there's steady money to be made
To help out 'twixt the harvest
And the tilling time.

The mate is spied in colloquy
And, quick surrounded,
Plied with ardent pleas.
He does not long demur:
The boat will shortly have a crew.

II

We progress further down the beach.
The mollusk shells lie scattered on the line
That marks the highest turning of the tide,
Their habitants long since the victims of
The questing gulls that circle overhead.
The seaweed sits in little piles
Beyond the water's edge.
We laugh and pop the bubbled sacs
That one time gave them buoyancy:
They will not need them now.
We detour slightly as we walk
So that the sandpipers are not disturbed,
And almost gratefully they do their act,
Pursuing the retreating tide
In search of bits of sustenance
Before they beat a swift retreat,
Outpacing the oncoming wave.
And idly one gives passing thought
That these so minute forms
The birds devour may have once been
Progenitors to all that ever lived.

Still further on a conch is found.
We lift it to our ears
To listen to the gentle roar,
An echo of the timeless tides,
The sad song of eternity.
But there is yet a peace about the scene
That slips the knots of nerves grown taut:
The tender breeze, the sweet salt smell,
The waves alapping on the shore.

So long ago it was.
These men with stubble on their chins
Learn quickly when they're young,
And daily practice sharpens skills.
They loose the boat from davit points
And catch it as it drops, in unison,
With measured rhythms of a sailor song.
The boat is heavy and their biceps bulge
But many hands make light of it,
Until it sits upright at just the water's edge.
They roll it out on time-smoothed logs,
And thrust it in the sea.
Impatiently its prowhead nods with every wave,
A thoroughbred before the race.

And all the while the mate observes
Them as they push and pull
And quickly clamber to their posts,
Assigned to each and each his own.
The oars they fit into the locks,

The strokes descend in harmony,
Each in a prescribed length,
Each at the proper angled tilt,
Each at a depth gauged by the practiced hand.
The forward arc is neatly timed,
Reentry in the surf a single slice, —
As pretty as the painting in the Manse.
Best not to praise too much too soon.

The waves dissemble, playing false,
Sometimes crossed and sometimes troughed,
Requiring quick reaction by all hands,
So that the bow meets breaker head to head.
Beware the sudden surge beneath;
The boat lifts vertically to top
The roller's spume before
It plunges down the trough
Created by the swelling surge.

Not once but many, many times
The willing craft performs its magic act:
To climb up, up, precariously,
Until it teeters on the top
Of stretching billows so the bottom
Of the boat shines white and glistens
In the sun before it swiftly drops
Down the next trough and disappears
Before triumphantly emerging
Once again.
Then suddenly the breakers level off.

From forward view and all about
There is naught but the swelling sea,
Its undulating rhythm leashed,
Deceptively concealing forces
Held prisoner by moon and wind and tide.

A moment only has the crew
To wipe from brows the sweat and spindrift
Gathered there, to stare across the blanket of
The awesome deep and feel
Its great immensity.

A spoken word and then reluctantly
The prow is pointed toward the distant shore,
Now but a bit of haze fast merging with the sea.
With quick half-strokes the crew responds,
Intent upon response to orders gauged
To catch the timing of the wave.
Commands are barked and all hands bend
To ride the wave before it breaks.
Again they teeter on the crest,
Then plunge in breathless haste
To glide to shallow depths
And feel the grating of the welcome sand.

All summer long the sun beats down
On bronzed and rippling muscles taut
With skill and discipline.
And there is prideful joy within their hearts,
The joy of sweet accomplishment
And mastery of forces of the deep.

III

The clanging of the iron ring
Suspended from the low-branched pine
Awakens those who live close by.
And they in turn make haste to pound
On doors that house the others of the crew.
Oilskins and boots are quickly donned
And quicker still are said goodbyes
To clinging mothers, wives before they dart
Into the night to brave
The tempest from the skies.
The boat is shortly launched,
The mate terse, upright in the stern
To face his crew
And guide them with commands
The wind tears from his salted lips.
The Keeper of the Light does well
To point the way with beacon shining bright
To where the rockets from the sinking ship
Bring brief illumination to the scene.

The story is not long to tell,
Though told it was a thousand times
At hearth and home and taverns where
Draughts were raised in memory.
A bark it was, square-rigged,
And settling by the bow.
A little crowd is gathered on the beach
With no protection but their gear

Against the pelting torrents
Lashed by tempestuous winds,
Whose ululations whine a dirge
That makes a mockery of puny man.
Anxious eyes upon the beach
Trace the light and glimpse the boat,
With crest outlined, encased in spume,
The walls of water, black on white,
Rising suddenly to lift the prow,
A featherweight, —so high, so high,
Then let it fall,
Scarce time to gather strength to meet
The challenge of the next cascade.
All this is stark outlined
Before the awe-struck crowd.

And then, quite suddenly, the boat soars high
And plunges down, obscured
In dark and sea and foam,
Into the vortex of the maelstrom's grasp,
Combining wind and rain and billowed might.
Both boat and men are lost to view
As though they never were.

The Light veers focus frantically
About the churning scene
As those on shore press to the water's edge
And gaze hard at the void
In vain attempt to conjure up
A vision of the boat and men.

But all they see is billowed froth
And blackness all about.

Capsized, is what they say who know,
And seek to comfort those whose ties
Are closer than the bonds of friends.
Two bodies next day wash ashore,
The boat found drifting bottom up.
There is an item in the city press
That weekend sixty miles away.

IV

Now hand-in-hand we daily walk the beach
Expectantly, as though to find
Some treasure trove that time forgot.
The beach in turn rewards us with
The multi-colored sand
Touched deep with minerals
That sparkle in the sun.
The sand in laminated weathering
Has formed ridged patterns like a fallen oak.
Piles of seaweed, hollowed shells
Proclaim marine mortality.
Frightened sandcrabs, caught off base,
Scurry to their burrowed sanctuary,
While sandhoppers, ignoring us,
In fury move minute sand mountains
Backward 'twixt their legs.

We laugh at them and saunter on.
Along the edges of the beach
The grasses vie with bushes weighed
With beach plums for the taking.
A solitary cloud plays wantonly
Before the climbing sun,
Its light mixed with the shadow
On the mirrored sea below.
The sun, the shade, the gentle roar
Are like a benediction in the breast
With peace enveloping
The heart and mind and all we see.

But then quite suddenly we come upon
A ship-shaped mound from which protrudes
A mast that slants upward to the sky.
A ship, we're told, 'twas wrecked
A century ago and dug its own grave
In the shifting sand.
We shake our heads and walk on by,
While only susurrations of the grass
And the sough of wind on water,
Whispering like conspirators,
Betray the stirring of an elemental force,
A darkling Presence near at hand.

Meanwhile tiny wavelets, playing leapfrog,
Lap softly on the shore.

August 1988

Christmas

Yes, Christmas is a special time
For merriment and cheer,
For icicles and tinkling bells
And starlight cold and clear,

For carols in the frosty air
And stockings hanging high,
For crowds around the punch bowl's brim
and neighbors coming by,

For twinkling lights to deck the tree
And presents piled beneath,
For decorations all about
Of mistletoe and wreath,

For Santa Claus and wonderment
And tiny tots' surprise,
For understanding, trust and love
Found in another's eyes,

For tables rich with tasty food
And fellowship combined,
For greetings from old friends and new,
Enhancing ties that bind,

For memories of Yuletides past
With those who are no more,
For thankfulness for health and home
And blessings by the score,

For gratitude to those who've tried
To help someone in need,
Who give of selves regardless of
One's color, race or creed,

For all the things the soul may seek
We search for as we pray,
That brotherhood of lasting peace
Be found on Christmas Day.

Christmas 1988

Shelley Plain

No need to have seen Shelley plain
To catch the moment beyond price,
The moment that sweet circumstance
Finds focus by some alchemy,
Transmuting mundane into ore
That's far more precious than the parts.

A moment fragile, gossamer,
Like evanescent dreams,
So quick to pass unmarked
Unless its timeless quality
Is clutched before it fades.

The moment beyond price indeed:
The eagle's feather and much more;
The fireside talk that coaxed,
Then overtook, the dawn;
The gnarled old pine that stood
In bold relief, self-etched
Against both sky and memory;
The thankful ignorance of last goodbyes;
The proffered hand extended in
A time of deep distress;
The group that joined in songs
As old as friendship's clasp.

Them all and more the miser mind
Collects to covet in the heart of hearts,
Accretions in the treasure lode
That form a lifelong heritage
And make the journey bitter-sweet.

Christmas 1988

Handprints Eight

These precious handprints, soon outgrown,
Recall the happiness we've known
Already in this dainty miss,
Who brings us challenge, pride and bliss.

Make no mistake: this little mite's
A powder keg of pure delights,
Whose piquant charms are cause for joy
Within the heart of any boy.

So self-assured, with poise endowed,
With feet on ground and head in cloud,
A graceful mix of substance, style,
Encaptured in a radiant smile.

So sweet, so kind, yet quick to lead,
To whom success seems guaranteed,
A product of love's melody
That's all enwrapped in Emily.

September 1989

SINGING THE BLUES AWAY

O, once there was a mighty Blue
Who knew all that most fishes knew.
From wave-crest to the ocean floor,
He knew the ancient piscean lore.

He knew the traps, the tides, the waves,
That swept his confreres to their graves.
He also knew of fishermen,
And was quite canny of their ken.

He knew their habits and their traits
And the flavor of their baits.
He knew that once a fish was hooked,
Very shortly he'd be cooked.

But then one day this mighty Blue,
While idly sipping salty brew,
Saw a strange object, jury-rigged;
Immediately he was intrigued.

Approaching slyly, he just snacked.
The taste was good; he soon attacked.
But soon he learned his big mistake:
The hook he grabbed was no cream cake.

At once he sank down to the bottom,
Where, he knew, few fishermen got 'em,
And when the line lay loose a little
He chewed and chewed it down the middle.

But the fisherman was also keen
And sensed the thought in Old Blue's bean.
He gave the line a mighty yank
That nearly cost Old Blue a shank.

And then began a fearful war,
Such as was rarely seen before.
Old Blue ran fast and then ran slow,
But the fisher seemed to know.

He reeled him in, then gave him slack;
Old Blue just feared he'd break his back.
He gave one last, astounding leap,
And crashed down on the deck, a heap.

The fisherman then knew what to do:
Wrap him in ice to keep him blue.
Hurry him home to a refrigerator
And grin about eating him later.

But when later came, no fish was found,
Not any trace upon the ground.
They looked on high; they looked on low,
Not even a scale was there to show.

It soon became a mystery,
And even a note for history.
TV had a story they said was true:
"Whatever happened to Old Blue?"

But there are those who say that they've heard
Of strangest legends and a whispered word,
Of hearing flipper sounds both night and day
That seem to lead to the Chesapeake Bay.

And there are greybeards down by the shore
Who twixt 'bacco chaws woke up and swore
That if you catch the moonbeams just, just right
And glint your eyes to squeeze the night,

Then watch for a wave to reach its peak,
Then see a shadowy piscine streak
High in the sky in a beauteous arc,
Proving its freedom just for a lark,

And then watch for the splash of brown and white
With a gorgeous flash of blue that might—
Just might—be that of Old Blue, back there to stay,
Singing just singing the blues away.

September 1989

Author's Notes

Editor's notes are in parentheses.

From 1925 to 1929

P. 4 *Green Years: Vignettes of Childhood*: This really belongs in a book of children's poetry. However, since they are sketches of childhood recollected in maturity, I doubt if they would be understood by small children or appeal to them.

P. 9 *The Letter She Never Received — Chink: (*Chink was the nickname of a college friend.)

From 1930 to 1933

P. 68 *Dream Castles*: "It is better to dream …." G.M.S. : (Gertrude Schneider was a member of the author's 1920's group of friends.)

P. 84 *In Memoriam — D.S.* : (Dave Siff, a boyhood friend, lost his life attempting to save another person's life.)

P. 110 *Sonnet to a Former Roommate:* Dedicated to E.D. and E.G. for the same yet different reasons.

From 1941 to 1954

P. 121 *On Reading John Donne:* While taking a course at New York University in Seventeenth Century English Literature, I came to admire the writings of John Donne, reading all his poetry and a lot more. His poems dealt generally with three subjects: women, death and religion. *On Reading John Donne* attempts to capture his basic premises on each of these subjects as well as to employ devices common to his style.

P. 123 *Some Things There Are:* Written at Camp Butner, North Carolina and Fort Benning, Georgia.

P. 125 *Sonnet to Moloch:* This was written during the war years when I was in the army. Its vituperative bitterness does not reflect any anti-war or pacifistic tendencies but rather a repulsion at the wanton waste of human life and the destructive characteristics of any war.

P. 126 *Testament to Marilyn:* This was written when she was one, to be read when she is one and twenty.

Like *Judas, Testament to Marilyn* was conceived during the long, hard months I spent in the Third Infantry Regiment at Camp Butner, North Carolina and Fort Benning, Georgia. Sometimes I would think of an idea while typing laundry lists in the supply room, sometimes while digging a foxhole in the field or while picking blackberries between mock skirmishes. More often it was conceived during the evenings in the sterile, smoke-filled raucous atmosphere of the company day room to the tune of clicking pool balls and boogie-woogie music from a scratchy radio. I enjoyed it, because it was a release from the present, but it left me mentally weary. The latter part of the poem was written during my months in the comparative calm of the

Academic Regiment day room or on a balcony overlooking the restful cuartel.

The original idea of the poem, like most germs, must have flourished unnoticed for a long time, for when I began to write, the ideas unfolded like rolling hills. My main trouble was that I wanted to advise and guide, and this frequently fell into preaching. Many a line has not survived for this reason, but some of it remains, inescapable in writing whose objective is to instruct.

I began the poem in blank verse and later changed it, rhyming the whole of the first half of it. But after consideration, I discarded the rhyme entirely, any remaining rhymes being inadvertently in the original.

It was a labor of love, if there ever was one. I wrote it when Marilyn was a year old and wanted her to read it when she could comprehend its meaning. I wish that I could have written something similar for the other children, but one never walks the same road twice.

P. 131 *Judas:* Of all the poems that I have written, I believe I consider *Judas* my most artistic attempt. It was written during the winter of 1943 – 44, when I was spending my days digging slit trenches in the mud of Camp Butner and Fort Benning, physically exhausted but mentally climbing a wall.

Evenings I read such diverse works as the *Kalavala* and *Gone with the Wind*, but felt the need to put my mind to something more creative. For some reason I fastened on the idea of writing about Judas, a character who had always fascinated me as an enigma. I had felt that the Christian explanation of the betrayal was a bit too obvious, that there was at least a possibility that the archtraitor had a better reason for his action than a few pieces of silver.

Anyhow, I set to work writing the poem with no more reference works than one that told me a bit about the Sanhedrin and the names of the two ponds outside Jerusalem. I understand there are works of fiction extant that give similar explanations of the action of Judas, but I have never read any of them.

Judas: A Monologue. It is the week of the Jewish Passover. Jesus and his followers have lately come to Jerusalem to celebrate the holy days. Pontius Pilate, the Roman ruler, stirs uneasily in the city, hoping that the holiday season will pass without major incident, despite the large throng that has gathered there. The Great Sanhedrin, the Jewish council of seventy-one, is also there, weighing the evidence against the Nazarene Jesus, who in their thinking, has blasphemously declared himself the Son of God. They would like to punish him, but fearing his popularity with the crowd, would like to apprehend him when he is alone.

Judas Iscariot, one of Jesus's disciples, feeling sorely disturbed, absents himself from the group of followers and goes to a hill overlooking the city. It is night, but he can see the reflected waters of Siloam and Gihon, two pools of water close by, and the city of Jerusalem, shining white in the moonlight, and dominated by the Temple.

This is the setting for the musing of the distraught Judas as he ponders aloud the fate of the Jewish nation.

P. 145 *High Tide*: This was obviously inspired by Matthew Arnold's immortal *Dover Beach*. Some day I would like to try my hand at a more mature attempt.

P. 150 *Plexus*: This was written sometime during the Fifties. Much later I read a poem by Conrad Aiken that was similar in theme. I recall that when I was in high school, Dave Siff wrote a short story about an aristocrat attempting to flee from the French Revolution. In his flight he came to a 'Y' in the road. The story details what would have happened if he had taken either of the two roads, or turned back, the end result being the same. It is possible he patterned his story after one by O. Henry which has similar development.

P. 154 *The Calling of General Moore:* (This was written to honor Major General Robert Scurlock Moore, U.S. Army, on the occasion of his retirement.)

FROM 1960 TO 1968

P. 163 *Cafeteria Blues:* (This was written as a get-well poem for a Senate Appropriations Committee colleague.)

P. 164 *Washington*: One day Mary discovered an invitation to a long-past embassy party buried under a pile of correspondence. At the time, such invitations were very frequent, but she regretted not having acknowledged it. Thus was born *Washington.*

P. 166 *Written for a Precious Moment*: (This was written on the author's birthday.)

P. 171 *Portrait:* I guess I worked on *Portrait* at intervals over a period of ten or fifteen years, finishing it sometime during the Sixties. I don't have any idea as to what prompted it; maybe nothing more than an admiring glance at Browning's *My Last Duchess.* If there is anything biographical in it, then it must be a collage type of remembrance of things past. Certainly it does not depict one individual, but maybe the amalgam of a lot of folks I came to know who rose to power.

P. 178 *The Silver Years:* (This was written on the author's 25th wedding anniversary.)

P. 181 *The Vase:* This is one of my favorites, although I certainly don't claim that it has any merit: if one person (even the author!) likes a poem, that is sufficient reason for having written it. My mother had such a vase on the living room wall, just as one would walk into the furnace room. I don't know what became of it.

P. 183 *Boarding House Blues:* It would be interesting to know how and why those of us who attempt to write bits of verse attempt to do so. *Boarding House Blues* is an example. A friend played a recording of some of Dylan Thomas' poetry. To him the poems were sheer magic. To us, his elders of another generation, they were that much balderdash. I devised a game. I wrote diverse nouns, verbs, adjectives and adverbs, each on a separate piece of paper. We put them in separate groups, and each of us drew one slip in each of the four categories. Having put them together in sentences, we read them aloud. Some of them hardly made any more sense than the efforts of Dylan Thomas. But others bore up remarkably well, better than Thomas' best, I thought. From those emerged the essence of *Boarding House Blues.*

P. 187 *On Reading Dorothy Eddy's Poems:* (Dorothy Eddy and her husband were close friends of the author and his wife in Virginia.)

P. 189 *On Reading Emily Dickinson:* Mary was asked by her book club to report on the poetry of Emily Dickinson. I volunteered to dig out as many of her poems as I could find in our anthologies and read them as I searched. *On Reading Emily Dickinson* is the result.

P. 191 *Haiku Poems:* The simplicity, originality, discipline, imaginative quality, and philosophic overtones of the Haiku poems found in me a receptive audience. These eight offerings are my own attempts in the field.

Haiku poetry is a strict form of Japanese verse consisting of three lines, the first and third being of five syllables, the second seven. The subject matter is limited to observations of nature, frequently with philosophic overtones.

From 1971 to 1979

P. 195 *A Commodious Ode:* Mary suggested that this bit of humor be called *A Commodious Ode*, certainly a stroke of genius. She had it copyrighted when she discovered people were copying the verse. It was by far the most popular thing I ever wrote, which will give you an idea of the merit of the rest of the poems. Except for one four-line stanza insertion, it was composed in about a half hour.

P. 196 *A Room with a View:* I don't know how I came to write *A Room with a View*. Sometime around 1960 I began it, then put it aside, only to complete it more than a decade later. I was primarily interested in man's attempt to grapple with his environment and the strictures encountered in attempting to attain the goals of life. After that, it just grew by itself, in a rather bleak manner. I was never happy with the ending.

P. 200 *Bicentennial Hymn:* This needs no explanation except to say that it does not reflect my broad view of America but only that narrow segment of our population which is critically destructive, thoughtlessly selfish or just plain stupid. Unfortunately, they are the most vocal!

P. 204 *Jigsaw Puzzle:* This is one of two poems—the other being *A Room with a View*—that just seemed to grow by themselves without much planning on my part. I can hear the reader mutter, "They show it!"

P. 211 *Last Leaf*: I had read Oliver Wendell Holmes' poem, and while I appreciated what Whittier had called his "unique compound of humor and pathos" in writing the poem, I felt that a human last leaf deserved something with a bit more sterling than pewter, a bit more stature than humor.

Outside my window there is an oak tree of considerable age. Each fall the other trees around it surrender their leaves to the approaching winter, and each year many of the leaves of the oak, now dark and dried, remain through the sleet and snows and wintry blasts. Only when the crocuses push up their heads and the buds begin to form on the oak do the leaves depart, unobtrusively, painlessly, almost without regret, one function fulfilled, another about to begin.

And so, with Holmes' poem as impetus and the leaves of yesteryear as inspiration, *Last Leaf* was written.

P. 213 *On Listening to Burton's "Ariel" Symphony*: I was struck by the diversity of opinion of those who with me had listened to the first rendition of Stephen Burton's "Ariel" Symphony, and after returning home that night, I immediately sat down to describe in poetic form my impressions of the work. I shortly realized that to be fair more than one reaction should be explored; from that, my four opinions gradually emerged. Since the poetry of Sylvia Plath is bound up inextricably in the Burton music, the two media are similarly fused in this poem.

Stephen D. Burton wrote his "Symphony No. 2 for Baritone and Orchestra" in 1974 at the instance of the

National Symphony Bicentennial Commission. Its world premiere was given on October 26, 1976 by the National Symphony Orchestra under the direction of Antol Dorati. Stephen Dickson was the soloist. In a sense the work might better have been entitled a concerto, since the importance of the meaning rests with the words, and the voice is used as a solo instrument throughout. In it, Burton compresses seven of Sylvia Plath's poems into the five movements, strongly dominating the effect of the music. Burton has said that he attempted an entirely new and revolutionary style, combining the tonality and forms of the past with the techniques of the twentieth century.

(The National Symphony Orchestra is based in Washington, D.C.)

P. 218 *Handprints:* I have written so many bits of versification for special occasions that I have long since lost count of their number and the content of most of them. It is just as well. *Handprints* is one of the better ones and is included for special reasons.

P. 219 *Friendship:* One night in 1977 I lay in bed coaxing Morpheus, and for no reason that I can fathom some lines of imagery began to fall into place. I got up, grabbed a pencil and paper and finished off *Friendship* in a few minutes. The morning light persuaded me to delete the first two lines and change four or five words. Otherwise it remains as it was scribbled that night before I forgot it.

P. 221 *Words:* I was always interested in words, and so I wrote a poem about them, which turned out to be not so much a tribute to words as a dissection of man's character.

P. 225 *The Pebbled Ridge:* Robert Frost's *The Death of the Hired Man* has long been a favorite of mine, although I doubt if I have read it since my college days. At that time I did memorize the eight-line passage beginning, "Part of a moon was falling down the west..." and thought it among the most beautiful bits of verse in the English language.

Several years ago, perhaps in the early Seventies, I began toying with the idea of writing something similar to Frost's poem. As I visualized it then, my poem would employ a dialogue involving a moral conflict between a husband and wife; it would be in blank verse; it would contain references to nature; and it would employ definitions of what home meant to the characters, in a word, all devices Frost used. All I needed, I believed, was a central theme, such as Frost's "Silas" problem. In my mind I developed several such themes but discarded them.

All this took time to nurture. It wasn't until 1976, some time after I had had the initial thought and more than forty years since I had read the poem, that I thought of the theme that I was to use in *The Pebbled Ridge,* although I originally entitled it *The Job.* As I wrote I several times thought of rereading Frost's poem, but successfully fought off the temptation. The man-wife conflict remains, as does the blank verse, and a bit of reference to natural surroundings. The coincidence of the idea in the opening lines was pure accident: I'm certain that no residue of memory inspired the similarity. I composed two definitions of home, but discarded them as unsuitable. Instead I substituted the definition of friendship.

The symbolism of pushing the pebbles with the foot was included almost at the last moment. I was troubled by it, still am, and rewrote the latter part of the poem three times. My first solution to the dilemma was implied rather than explicit and was subject to the possibility of being overlooked. I wanted the decision to be made before the phone call—that was the whole point of the story—but I did not want it to be too obvious, at least to her. The second version was straightforward, but did not seem to have a definite conclusion. The third version makes no bones about his decision but loses any subtlety. All three versions employed a device, not exactly a *deus ex machina*, but something akin to it.

I avoided Frost's unevenness of line and meter and tried to limit prosaic dialogue. I wanted the poem to employ sentiment without mawkishness, a thin line to walk. The reader will have to decide for himself whether or not I was successful. There are some lines in the poem that I like, and some that may even be overwritten, but none to compare with those eight lines that Frost wrote!

P. 235 *Boundary Brook:* When my granddaughter Meredith Anderson was two years old, she was given an illustrated copy of Robert Frost's *Stopping by Woods on a Snowy Evening*. She liked both poem and illustrations, and often would ask us to read it to her, which we did.

After one such occasion, I was mentally propelled—there is no other way to describe it—to see what I could do in somewhat the same vein. I wanted it to be enough like Frost's poems so that the reader might recognize a similarity, yet be completely original. Obviously such a poem must have a rhymed pattern and must deal with nature. It must be simple and yet carry a not-too-obvious undertone of meaning as well.

This proved to be a rather tall order. How well I succeeded, the reader can judge for himself.

P. 237 *The Wreck of the Nancy Lee:* I began *The Wreck of the Nancy Lee* when I was a boy, but never got very far with it. Some fifty years or so later I found three or four verses from it and decided to finish it in much the same vein as I had started it so long ago. With no pretensions of literary accomplishment to worry about, I just had fun with it.

FROM 1980 TO 1989

P. 260 *On Reading Kristen's Poetry:* (This poetry by Kristen McCracken, daughter of the author's long-time family friend, was written when she was a teenager.)

P. 263 *This Day*: This has no inspirational source other than the rising of the sun and the beauty that is unfolded with each passing day, something that we perhaps are too busy to fully recognize and appreciate. This is true not only of the marvelous mystery of the physical world but also of the splendor inherent in human relationships were we to suppress the reserve built up through millennia of societal protectivism.

P. 266 *Les Roses du Septembre*: In appreciation of André Maurois.

P. 267 *Five Mile Beach*: (This poem was inspired by the historic Hereford Inlet Lighthouse, North Wildwood, New Jersey. The author's great-uncle was Keeper of the Light for 40 years.)

P. 283 *Singing the Blues Away*: or Scaling the Blue Notes.

A Note About the Author

Francis S. Hewitt was born in Atlantic City, New Jersey, in 1909 and grew up in Ventnor City.

He earned his undergraduate and master's degrees in English from Rutgers University and did further postgraduate work in English at New York University.

In 1942 he moved to Washington, D.C., to join the staff of the Joint Committee on Reduction of Non-Essential Federal Expenditures, headed by Senator Harry F. Byrd.

He served in the army during the final years of World War II, then returned to the Byrd Committee as staff director. In 1947 he joined the Senate Appropriations Committee staff and retired in 1974 as director of the Senate Appropriations Defense Sub-Committee. In 1967, he wrote the centennial history of the Senate Appropriations Committee.

Throughout his life, he wrote poetry. In his eightieth year, he wrote to friends: "Having been raised within sight of the breakers, I am prejudiced in favor of the smell of the salt and the sound of the waves." His last poem before his death in 1990 related to the sea.

He and his wife Mary lived in Arlington, Virginia. They are the parents of three children and the grandparents of four.

Colophon

Editing by Caroline J. Jackson
Design by J. Robert Capps
Pen and ink drawing, Hereford Inlet Lighthouse,
by Edwin M. Hewitt
Jacket cover, color monotype
by Priscilla Treacy
Composition in Macintosh QuarkXPress
Typeface, Adobe Palatino
Printing by Bookcrafters
via offset lithography
on 60# Booktext Natural